Cram101 Textbook Outlines to accompany:

Biopsychology

Pinel, 6th Edition

An Academic Internet Publishers (AIPI) publication (c) 2007.

With Cram101.com online, you also have access to extensive reference material.

You will nail those essays and papers. Here is an example from a Cram101 Biology text:

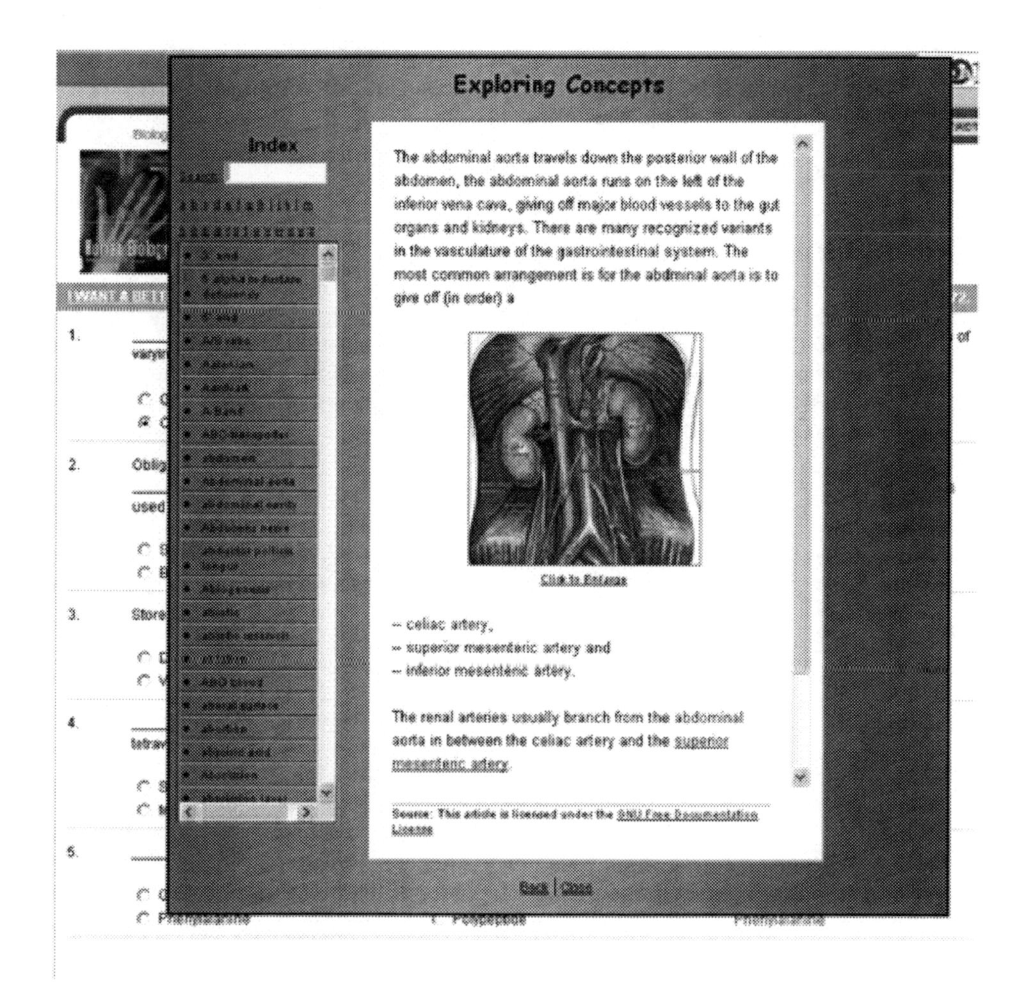

Visit **www.Cram101.com**, click Sign Up at the top of the screen, and enter DK73DW3586 in the promo code box on the registration screen. Access to www.Cram101.com is normally $9.95, but because you have purchased this book, your access fee is only $4.95. Sign up and stop highlighting textbooks forever.

Learning System

Cram101 Textbook Outlines is a learning system. The notes in this book are the highlights of your textbook, you will never have to highlight a book again.

How to use this book. Take this book to class, it is your notebook for the lecture. The notes and highlights on the left hand side of the pages follow the outline and order of the textbook. All you have to do is follow along while your intructor presents the lecture. Circle the items emphasized in class and add other important information on the right side. With Cram101 Textbook Outlines you'll spend less time writing and more time listening. Learning becomes more efficient.

Cram101.com Online

Increase your studying efficiency by using Cram101.com's practice tests and online reference material. It is the perfect complement to Cram101 Textbook Outlines. Use self-teaching matching tests or simulate in-class testing with comprehensive multiple choice tests, or simply use Cram's true and false tests for quick review. Cram101.com even allows you to enter your in-class notes for an integrated studying format combining the textbook notes with your class notes.

Visit **www.Cram101.com**, click Sign Up at the top of the screen, and enter **DK73DW3586** in the promo code box on the registration screen. Access to www.Cram101.com is normally $9.95, but because you have purchased this book, your access fee is only $4.95. Sign up and stop highlighting textbooks forever.

 The Cram101 Textbook Outline series is printed in the United States. ISBN: 1-4288-1312-8

Biopsychology
Pinel, 6th

CONTENTS

Pinel	Pinel is regarded as the father of modern psychiatry. He was a clinician believing that medical truth derived from clinical experience. While at Bicêtre, Pinel did away with bleeding, purging, and blistering in favor a therapy that involved close contact with and careful observation of patients.
Neuron	The neuron is the primary cell of the nervous system. They are found in the brain, the spinal cord, in the nerves and ganglia of the peripheral nervous system. It is a specialized cell that conducts impulses through the nervous system and contains three major parts: cell body, dendrites, and an axon. It can have many dendrites but only one axon.
Brain	The brain controls and coordinates most movement, behavior and homeostatic body functions such as heartbeat, blood pressure, fluid balance and body temperature. Functions of the brain are responsible for cognition, emotion, memory, motor learning and other sorts of learning. The brain is primarily made up of two types of cells: glia and neurons.
Attention	Attention is the cognitive process of selectively concentrating on one thing while ignoring other things. Psychologists have labeled three types of attention: sustained attention, selective attention, and divided attention.
Biopsychology	Biopsychology is the scientific study of the biological bases of behavior and mental states. Empirical experiments study changes in central nervous system activation in response to a stimulus.
Biopsychologist	A psychologist who studies the relationship between behavior and biological processes, especially activity in the nervous system is referred to as a Biopsychologist.
Evolution	Commonly used to refer to gradual change, evolution is the change in the frequency of alleles within a population from one generation to the next. This change may be caused by different mechanisms, including natural selection, genetic drift, or changes in population (gene flow).
Species	Species refers to a reproductively isolated breeding population.
Insight	Insight refers to a sudden awareness of the relationships among various elements that had previously appeared to be independent of one another.
Evolutionary perspective	A perspective that focuses on how humans have evolved and adapted behaviors required for survival against various environmental pressures over the long course is called the evolutionary perspective.
Neuroscience	A field that combines the work of psychologists, biologists, biochemists, medical researchers, and others in the study of the structure and function of the nervous system is neuroscience.
Perception	Perception is the process of acquiring, interpreting, selecting, and organizing sensory information.
Motivation	In psychology, motivation is the driving force (desire) behind all actions of an organism.
Learning	Learning is a relatively permanent change in behavior that results from experience. Thus, to attribute a behavioral change to learning, the change must be relatively permanent and must result from experience.
Emotion	An emotion is a mental states that arise spontaneously, rather than through conscious effort. They are often accompanied by physiological changes.
Hebb	Hebb demonstrated that the rearing of rats in an enriched environment could alter neural development and that sensory - neural connections were shaped by experience. He is famous for developing the concept of neural nets. He also believed that learning early in life is of the incremental variety, whereas later it is cognitive, insightful, and more all-or-none.
Physiology	The study of the functions and activities of living cells, tissues, and organs and of the physical and chemical phenomena involved is referred to as physiology.
Case study	A carefully drawn biography that may be obtained through interviews, questionnaires, and psychological tests is called a case study.
Nervous system	The body's electrochemical communication circuitry, made up of billions of neurons is a nervous system.

Neurochemistry	Neurochemistry is a branch of neuroscience that is heavily devoted to the study of neurochemicals. A neurochemical is an organic molecule that participates in neural activity. This term is often used to refer to neurotransmitters and other molecules such as neuro-active drugs that influence neuron function.
Subjective experience	Subjective experience refers to reality as it is perceived and interpreted, not as it exists objectively.
Paradoxical	Paradoxical intention refers to instructing clients to do the opposite of the desired behavior. Telling an impotent man not to have sex or an insomniac not to sleep reduces anxiety to perform.
Variable	A variable refers to a measurable factor, characteristic, or attribute of an individual or a system.
Independent variable	A condition in a scientific study that is manipulated (assigned different values by a researcher) so that the effects of the manipulation may be observed is called an independent variable.
Dependent variable	A measure of an assumed effect of an independent variable is called the dependent variable.
Alcoholism	A disorder that involves long-term, repeated, uncontrolled, compulsive, and excessive use of alcoholic beverages and that impairs the drinker's health and work and social relationships is called alcoholism.
Alcoholic	An alcoholic is dependent on alcohol as characterized by craving, loss of control, physical dependence and withdrawal symptoms, and tolerance.
Applied research	Applied research is done to solve specific, practical questions; its primary aim is not to gain knowledge for its own sake. It can be exploratory but often it is descriptive. It is almost always done on the basis of basic research.
Pure research	Pure research is conducted without concern for immediate applications.
Motives	Needs or desires that energize and direct behavior toward a goal are motives.
Society	The social sciences use the term society to mean a group of people that form a semi-closed (or semi-open) social system, in which most interactions are with other individuals belonging to the group.
Physiological psychology	Physiological psychology refers to the study of the physiological mechanisms, in the brain and elsewhere, that mediate behavior and psychological experiences.
Theories	Theories are logically self-consistent models or frameworks describing the behavior of a certain natural or social phenomenon. They are broad explanations and predictions concerning phenomena of interest.
Psychopharma-ology	Psychopharmacology refers to the study of the effects of drugs on the mind and on behavior; also known as medication and drug therapy.
Neuropsychology	Neuropsychology is a branch of psychology that aims to understand how the structure and function of the brain relates to specific psychological processes.
Cerebral hemisphere	Either of the two halves that make up the cerebrum is referred to as a cerebral hemisphere. The hemispheres operate together, linked by the corpus callosum, a very large bundle of nerve fibers, and also by other smaller commissures.
Cerebral cortex	The cerebral cortex is the outermost layer of the cerebrum and has a grey color. It is made up of four lobes and it is involved in many complex brain functions including memory, perceptual awareness, "thinking", language and consciousness. The cerebral cortex receives sensory information from many different sensory organs eg: eyes, ears, etc. and processes the information.
Neuropsychol-gical test	A neuropsychological test use specifically designed tasks used to measure a psychological function known to be linked to a particular brain structure or pathway. They usually involve the systematic administration of clearly defined procedures in a formal environment.

Left hemisphere	The left hemisphere of the cortex controls the right side of the body, coordinates complex movements, and, in 95% of people, controls the production of speech and written language.
Psychophysiology	Psychophysiology is the science of understanding the link between psychology and physiology. Psychophysiology is different from physiological psychology in that psychophysiology looks at the way psychological activities produce physiological responses, while physiological psychology looks at the physiological mechanisms which lead to psychological activity.
Pupil	In the eye, the pupil is the opening in the middle of the iris. It appears black because most of the light entering it is absorbed by the tissues inside the eye. The size of the pupil is controlled by involuntary contraction and dilation of the iris, in order to regulate the intensity of light entering the eye. This is known as the pupillary reflex.
Autonomic nervous system	A division of the peripheral nervous system, the autonomic nervous system, regulates glands and activities such as heartbeat, respiration, digestion, and dilation of the pupils. It is responsible for homeostasis, maintaining a relatively constant internal environment .
Electroencep-alogram	Electroencephalography is the neurophysiologic measurement of the electrical activity of the brain by recording from electrodes placed on the scalp, or in the special cases on the cortex. The resulting traces are known as an electroencephalogram and represent so-called brainwaves.
Information processing	Information processing is an approach to the goal of understanding human thinking. The essence of the approach is to see cognition as being essentially computational in nature, with mind being the software and the brain being the hardware.
Cognition	The intellectual processes through which information is obtained, transformed, stored, retrieved, and otherwise used is cognition.
Visual cortex	The visual cortex is the general term applied to both the primary visual cortex and the visual association area. Anatomically, the visual cortex occupies the entire occipital lobe, the inferior temporal lobe (IT), posterior parts of the parietal lobe, and a few small regions in the frontal lobe.
Pathology	Pathology is the study of the processes underlying disease and other forms of illness, harmful abnormality, or dysfunction.
Comparative psychology	Comparative psychology is the study of the behavior of animals in order to infer similar functionaility in humans.
Ethology	Where comparative psychology sees the study of animal behavior in the context of what is known about human psychology, ethology sees the study of animal behavior in the context of what is known about animal anatomy and physiology.
Ecology	Ecology refers to the branch of biology that deals with the relationships between living organisms and their environment.
Genetics	Genetics is the science of genes, heredity, and the variation of organisms.
Comparative psychologist	A comparative psychologist is primarily interested in studying and comparing the behavior of different species.
Brain imaging	Brain imaging is a fairly recent discipline within medicine and neuroscience. Brain imaging falls into two broad categories -- structural imaging and functional imaging.
Acetylcholine	The chemical compound acetylcholine was the first neurotransmitter to be identified. It plays a role in learning, memory, and rapid eye movement sleep and causes the skeletal muscle fibers to contract.
Neurotransmitter	A neurotransmitter is a chemical that is used to relay, amplify and modulate electrical signals between a neurons and another cell.
Hippocampus	The hippocampus is a part of the brain located inside the temporal lobe. It forms a part of the limbic system and plays a part in memory and navigation.

Syndrome	The term syndrome is the association of several clinically recognizable features, signs, symptoms, phenomena or characteristics which often occur together, so that the presence of one feature indicates the presence of the others.
Thiamine	Thiamine, also known as vitamin B1, is a colorless compound with chemical formula $C_{12}H_{17}ClN_4OS$. Systemic thiamine deficiency can lead to myriad problems including neurodegeneration, wasting, and death. Well-known syndromes caused by lack of thiamine due to malnutrition or a diet high in thiaminase-rich foods include Wernicke-Korsakoff syndrome and beriberi, diseases also common in chronic abusers of alcohol.
Metabolism	Metabolism is the biochemical modification of chemical compounds in living organisms and cells.
Inference	Inference is the act or process of drawing a conclusion based solely on what one already knows.
Scientific method	Psychologists gather data in order to describe, understand, predict, and control behavior. Scientific method refers to an approach that can be used to discover accurate information. It includes these steps: understand the problem, collect data, draw conclusions, and revise research conclusions.
Empirical	Empirical means the use of working hypotheses which are capable of being disproved using observation or experiment.
Retina	The retina is a thin layer of cells at the back of the eyeball. It is the part of the eye which converts light into nervous signals. The retina contains photoreceptor cells which receive the light; the resulting neural signals then undergo complex processing by other neurons of the retina, and are transformed into action potentials in retinal ganglion cells whose axons form the optic nerve.
Curare	Curare is a drug that once entered into the bloodstream and reaches the muscles it blocks the receptors on the muscles, paralyzing the muscles.
Homosexuality	Homosexuality refers to a sexual orientation characterized by aesthetic attraction, romantic love, and sexual desire exclusively for members of the same sex or gender identity.
Schizophrenia	Schizophrenia is characterized by persistent defects in the perception or expression of reality. A person suffering from untreated schizophrenia typically demonstrates grossly disorganized thinking, and may also experience delusions or auditory hallucinations
Morphine	Morphine, the principal active agent in opium, is a powerful opioid analgesic drug. According to recent research, it may also be produced naturally by the human brain. Morphine is usually highly addictive, and tolerance and physical and psychological dependence develop quickly.
Feedback	Feedback refers to information returned to a person about the effects a response has had.
Gene	A gene is an ultramicroscopic area of the chromosome. It is the smallest physical unit of the DNA molecule that carries a piece of hereditary information.
Critical thinking	Critical thinking is a mental process of analyzing or evaluating information, particularly statements or propositions that are offered as true.
Electrode	Any device used to electrically stimulate nerve tissue or to record its activity is an electrode.
Nucleus	In neuroanatomy, a cluster of cell bodies of neurons within the central nervous system is a nucleus.
Caudate nucleus	The caudate nucleus is a telencephalic nucleus, one of the input nuclei of the basal ganglia; involved with control of voluntary movement in the brain.
Behavioral observation	A form of behavioral assessment that entails careful observation of a person's overt behavior in a particular situation is behavioral observation.
Mental illness	Mental illness is the term formerly used to mean psychological disorder but less preferred because it implies that the causes of the disorder can be found in a medical disease process.
Lobotomy	A lobotomy is the intentional severing of the prefrontal cortex from the thalamic region of the brain.

The frontal lobe of the brain controls a number of advanced cognitive functions, as well as motor control. Today, lobotomy is very infrequently practised. It may be a treatment of last resort for obsessive-compulsive sufferers, and may also be used for people suffering chronic pain.

Lobes

The four major sections of the cerebral cortex: frontal, parietal, temporal, and occipital are called lobes.

Moniz

Moniz was the inventor of the frontal lobotomy as a surgical approach to the radical treatment of several kinds of mental diseases.

Lesion

A lesion is a non-specific term referring to abnormal tissue in the body. It can be caused by any disease process including trauma (physical, chemical, electrical), infection, neoplasm, metabolic and autoimmune.

Psychosurgery

Psychosurgery is a term for surgeries of the brain or autonomic nervous system involving the severance of neural pathways to effect a change in behavior, usually to treat or alleviate severe mental illness. The procedures typically considered psychosurgery are now almost universally shunned as inappropriate, due in part to the emergence of less-invasive methods of treatment such as psychiatric medication.

Frontal lobe

The frontal lobe comprises four major folds of cortical tissue: the precentral gyrus, superior gyrus and the middle gyrus of the frontal gyri, the inferior frontal gyrus. It has been found to play a part in impulse control, judgement, language, memory, motor function, problem solving, sexual behavior, socialization and spontaneity.

Epilepsy

Epilepsy is a chronic neurological condition characterized by recurrent unprovoked neural discharges. It is commonly controlled with medication, although surgical methods are used as well.

Zeitgeist

Zeitgeist, originally a German expression, means "the spirit of the time". It denotes the intellectual and cultural climate of an era.

Dichotomy

A dichotomy is the division of a proposition into two parts which are both mutually exclusive – i.e. both cannot be simultaneously true – and jointly exhaustive – i.e. they cover the full range of possible outcomes. They are often contrasting and spoken of as "opposites".

Biopsychology	Biopsychology is the scientific study of the biological bases of behavior and mental states. Empirical experiments study changes in central nervous system activation in response to a stimulus.
Brain	The brain controls and coordinates most movement, behavior and homeostatic body functions such as heartbeat, blood pressure, fluid balance and body temperature. Functions of the brain are responsible for cognition, emotion, memory, motor learning and other sorts of learning. The brain is primarily made up of two types of cells: glia and neurons.
Descartes	Descartes was concerned with the sharp contrast between the certainty of mathematics and the controversial nature of philosophy, and came to believe that the sciences could be made to yield results as certain as those of mathematics. He introduced the method of rationalism for arriving at knowledge. He also saw the human condition as a competition between the body and soul, introducing the concept of dualism.
Dualism	Dualism is a set of beliefs which begins with the claim that the mental and the physical have a fundamentally different nature. It is contrasted with varying kinds of monism, including materialism and phenomenalism. Dualism is one answer to the mind-body problem.
Cartesian dualism	Cartesian dualism was Descartes's principle of the separation of mind and matter and mind and body. The mind, according to Descartes, was a "thinking thing", and an immaterial substance. This "thing" was the essence of himself, the part that doubts, believes, hopes, and so on. The body is a material substance.
Dichotomy	A dichotomy is the division of a proposition into two parts which are both mutually exclusive – i.e. both cannot be simultaneously true – and jointly exhaustive – i.e. they cover the full range of possible outcomes. They are often contrasting and spoken of as "opposites".
Behaviorism	The school of psychology that defines psychology as the study of observable behavior and studies relationships between stimuli and responses is called behaviorism. Behaviorism relied heavily on animal research and stated the same principles governed the behavior of both nonhumans and humans.
Learning	Learning is a relatively permanent change in behavior that results from experience. Thus, to attribute a behavioral change to learning, the change must be relatively permanent and must result from experience.
Nurture	Nurture refers to the environmental influences on behavior due to nutrition, culture, socioeconomic status, and learning.
Watson	Watson, the father of behaviorism, developed the term "Behaviorism" as a name for his proposal to revolutionize the study of human psychology in order to put it on a firm experimental footing.
Trait	An enduring personality characteristic that tends to lead to certain behaviors is called a trait. The term trait also means a genetically inherited feature of an organism.
Ethology	Where comparative psychology sees the study of animal behavior in the context of what is known about human psychology, ethology sees the study of animal behavior in the context of what is known about animal anatomy and physiology.
Experimental psychology	Experimental psychology is an approach to psychology that treats it as one of the natural sciences, and therefore assumes that it is susceptible to the experimental method.
Species	Species refers to a reproductively isolated breeding population.
La Mettrie	La Mettrie is one of the founders of cognitive science. During an attack of fever he made observations on himself, which led him to the conclusion that psychical phenomena were to be accounted for as the effects of organic changes in the brain and nervous system.

Parietal lobe	The parietal lobe is positioned above (superior to) the occipital lobe and behind (posterior to) the frontal lobe. It plays important roles in integrating sensory information from various senses, and in the manipulation of objects.
Attention	Attention is the cognitive process of selectively concentrating on one thing while ignoring other things. Psychologists have labeled three types of attention: sustained attention, selective attention, and divided attention.
Anesthesia	Anesthesia is the process of blocking the perception of pain and other sensations. This allows patients to undergo surgery and other procedures without the distress and pain they would otherwise experience.
Comparative psychology	Comparative psychology is the study of the behavior of animals in order to infer similar functionaility in humans.
Genetics	Genetics is the science of genes, heredity, and the variation of organisms.
Premise	A premise is a statement presumed true within the context of a discourse, especially of a logical argument.
Gene	A gene is an ultramicroscopic area of the chromosome. It is the smallest physical unit of the DNA molecule that carries a piece of hereditary information.
Neuron	The neuron is the primary cell of the nervous system. They are found in the brain, the spinal cord, in the nerves and ganglia of the peripheral nervous system. It is a specialized cell that conducts impulses through the nervous system and contains three major parts: cell body, dendrites, and an axon. It can have many dendrites but only one axon.
Perception	Perception is the process of acquiring, interpreting, selecting, and organizing sensory information.
Nervous system	The body's electrochemical communication circuitry, made up of billions of neurons is a nervous system.
Evolution	Commonly used to refer to gradual change, evolution is the change in the frequency of alleles within a population from one generation to the next. This change may be caused by different mechanisms, including natural selection, genetic drift, or changes in population (gene flow).
Darwin	Darwin achieved lasting fame as originator of the theory of evolution through natural selection. His book Expression of Emotions in Man and Animals is generally considered the first text on comparative psychology.
Origin of Species	The Origin of Species by Charles Darwin makes the argument that groups of organisms gradually evolve through the process of natural selection. Characteristics that favor survival and reproduction are passed on to the next generation, those that do not, are gradually lost.
Selective breeding	Selective breeding refers to the mating of those members of a strain of animals or plants that manifest a particular characteristic, which may or may not be done deliberately, to affect the genetic makeup of future generations of that strain.
Natural selection	Natural selection is a process by which biological populations are altered over time, as a result of the propagation of heritable traits that affect the capacity of individual organisms to survive and reproduce.
Zeitgeist	Zeitgeist, originally a German expression, means "the spirit of the time". It denotes the intellectual and cultural climate of an era.
Empirical	Empirical means the use of working hypotheses which are capable of being disproved using observation or experiment.
Metaphor	A metaphor is a rhetorical trope where a comparison is made between two seemingly unrelated

	subjects
Mutation	Mutation is a permanent, sometimes transmissible (if the change is to a germ cell) change to the genetic material (usually DNA or RNA) of a cell. They can be caused by copying errors in the genetic material during cell division and by exposure to radiation, chemicals, or viruses, or can occur deliberately under cellular control during the processes such as meiosis or hypermutation.
Adaptation	Adaptation is a lowering of sensitivity to a stimulus following prolonged exposure to that stimulus. Behavioral adaptations are special ways a particular organism behaves to survive in its natural habitat.
Scrotum	The scrotum is an external sack of skin that holds the testes.
Spandrels	In evolutionary psychology, spandrels are phenotypic characteristics that evolved as a side effect of a true adaptation.
Umbilical cord	The umbilical cord is a tube that connects a developing embryo or fetus to its placenta. It contains major arteries and veins for the exchange of nutrient- and oxygen-rich blood between the embryo and placenta.
Brain stem	The brain stem is the stalk of the brain below the cerebral hemispheres. It is the major route for communication between the forebrain and the spinal cord and peripheral nerves. It also controls various functions including respiration, regulation of heart rhythms, and primary aspects of sound localization.
Cerebrum	The cerebrum (the portion of the brain that performs motor and sensory functions and a variety of mental activities) is divided into four lobes - the frontal, temporal, parietal and occipital lobes.
Trivers	Trivers is most noted for proposing the theories of reciprocal altruism, parental investment, and parent-offspring conflict. Other areas in which he has made influential contributions include an adaptive view of self-deception and intragenomic conflict.
Polygyny	Polygyny is a marital practice in which a man has more than one wife simultaneously.
Polyandry	A mating system in which each female seeks to mate with multiple males, while each male mates with only one female is referred to as polyandry.
Theories	Theories are logically self-consistent models or frameworks describing the behavior of a certain natural or social phenomenon. They are broad explanations and predictions concerning phenomena of interest.
Evolutionary psychology	Evolutionary psychology proposes that cognition and behavior can be better understood in light of evolutionary history.
Evolutionary theory	Evolutionary theory is concerned with heritable variability rather than behavioral variations. Natural selection requirements: (1) natural variability within a species must exist, (2) only some individual differences are heritable, and (3) natural selection only takes place when there is an interaction between the inborn attributes of organisms and the environment in which they live.
Physical attractiveness	Physical attractiveness is the perception of an individual as physically beautiful by other people.
Mendel	Mendel is often called the "father of genetics" for his study of the inheritance of traits in pea plants. Mendel showed that there was particulate inheritance of traits according to his laws of inheritance.
Phenotype	The phenotype of an individual organism is either its total physical appearance and constitution, or a specific manifestation of a trait, such as size or eye color, that varies

between individuals. Phenotype is determined to some extent by genotype, or by the identity of the alleles that an individual carries at one or more positions on the chromosomes.

Genotype — The genotype is the specific genetic makeup of an individual, usually in the form of DNA. It codes for the phenotype of that individual. Any given gene will usually cause an observable change in an organism, known as the phenotype.

Heterozygous — Heterozygous refers to the condition in which a pair of genes occupying the same locus on a pair of chromosomes are different from one another.

Homozygous — When an organism is referred to as being homozygous for a specific gene, it means that it carries two identical copies of that gene for a given trait on the two corresponding chromosomes (e.g., the genotype is AA or aa). Such a cell or an organism is called a homozygote.

Allele — An allele is any one of a number of alternative forms of the same gene (sometimes the term refers to a non-gene sequence) occupying a given locus (position) on a chromosome.

Chromosome — The DNA which carries genetic information in biological cells is normally packaged in the form of one or more large macromolecules called a chromosome. Humans normally have 46.

Nucleus — In neuroanatomy, a cluster of cell bodies of neurons within the central nervous system is a nucleus.

Gametes — Gametes are the specialized cells that come together during fertilization (conception) in organisms that reproduce sexually. In those species that produce two morphologically distinct types of gametes, and in which a particular individual produces only one type, "females" of the species produce the larger gamete called an ovum (or egg) and "males" produce the smaller gamete termed (in animals) a spermatozoon (or sperm).

Meiosis — The process of cell doubling and separation of chromosomes in which each pair of chromosomes in a cell separates, with one member of each pair going into each gamete is called meiosis.

Mitosis — Mitosis is the process by which a cell separates its duplicated genome into two identical halves.

Zygote — A zygote is a cell that is the result of fertilization. That is, two haploid cells—usually (but not always) a sperm cell from a male and an ovum from a female—merge into a single diploid cell called the zygote.

Sex chromosomes — The sex chromosomes are the 23rd pair of chromosomes. They determine whether the child will be male or female. A pair with two X-shaped chromosomes produces a female. A pair with an X chromosome and a Y chromosome produces a male.

X chromosome — The sex chromosomes are one of the 23 pairs of human chromosomes. Each person normally has one pair of sex chromosomes in each cell. Females have two X chromosomes, while males have one X and one Y chromosome. The X chromosome carries hundreds of genes but few, if any, of these have anything to do directly with sex determination.

Y chromosome — The Y chromosome is one of the two sex chromosomes in humans and most other mammals. The sex chromosomes are one of the 23 pairs of human chromosomes. The Y chromosome contains the fewest genes of any of the chromosomes. It contains the genes that cause testis development, thus determining maleness. It is usually contributed by the father.

Dominant gene — In genetics, the term dominant gene refers to the allele that causes a phenotype that is seen in a heterozygous genotype.

Recessive gene — Recessive gene refers to an allele that causes a phenotype (visible or detectable characteristic) that is only seen in a homozygous genotype (an organism that has two copies of the same allele). Thus, both parents have to be carriers of a recessive trait in order for

a child to express that trait.

Color blindness Color blindness in humans is the inability to perceive differences between some or all colors that other people can distinguish. It is most often of genetic nature, but may also occur because of eye, nerve, or brain damage, or due to exposure to certain chemicals.

Nucleotide A nucleotide is a monomer or the structural unit of nucleotide chains forming nucleic acids as RNA and DNA. They also play important roles in cellular energy transport and transformations and in enzyme regulation.

Deoxyribonuc-eic acid Deoxyribonucleic acid contains the genetic instructions specifying the biological development of all cellular forms of life. It is often referred to as the molecule of heredity, as it is responsible for the genetic propagation of most inherited traits.

Genetic code The genetic code is a set of rules, which maps DNA sequences to proteins in the living cell, and is employed in the process of protein synthesis. Nearly all living things use the same genetic code, called the standard genetic code, although a few organisms use minor variations of the standard code.

Protein A protein is a complex, high-molecular-weight organic compound that consists of amino acids joined by peptide bonds. It is essential to the structure and function of all living cells and viruses. Many are enzymes or subunits of enzymes.

Amino acid Amino acid is the basic structural building unit of proteins. They form short polymer chains called peptides or polypeptides which in turn form structures called proteins.

Hair cells Hair cells are the sensory cells of both the auditory system and the vestibular system. The auditory hair cells are located within the organ of Corti on a thin basilar membrane in the cochlea of the inner ear.

Cytoplasm Cytoplasm is the colloidal, semi-fluid matter contained within the cell's plasma membrane, in which organelles are suspended. In contrast to the protoplasm, the cytoplasm does not include the cell nucleus, the interior of which is made up of nucleoplasm.

Ribosome A ribosome is an organelle composed of rRNA and ribosomal proteins. It translates mRNA into a polypeptide chain (e.g., a protein). It can be thought of as a factory that builds a protein from a set of genetic instructions.

Mitochondria Mitochondria are sometimes described as "cellular power plants", because their primary function is to convert organic materials into energy in the form of ATP.

Human genome The complete sequence or mapping of genes in the human body and their locations is the human genome. It is made up of 23 chromosome pairs with a total of about 3 billion DNA base pairs.

Human genome project The Human Genome Project endeavored to map the human genome down to the nucleotide (or base pair) level and to identify all the genes present in it.

Heterogeneous A heterogeneous compound, mixture, or other such object is one that consists of many different items, which are often not easily sorted or separated, though they are clearly distinct.

Phenylalanine Phenylalanine is an essential amino acid. The genetic disorder phenylketonuria is an inability to metabolize phenylalanine.

Homozygote Homozygote cells are diploid or polyploid and have the same alleles at a locus (position) on homologous chromosomes. When an organism is referred to as being homozygous for a specific gene, it means that it carries two identical copies of that gene for a given trait on the two corresponding chromosomes. Such a cell or an organism is called a homozygote.

Mental retardation Mental retardation refers to having significantly below-average intellectual functioning and limitations in at least two areas of adaptive functioning. Many categorize retardation as

	mild, moderate, severe, or profound.
Sensitive period	A sensitive period is a developmental window in which a predisposed behavior is most likely to develop given appropriate stimulation. In linguistic theory, the period from about 18 months to puberty is when the brain is thought to be primed for learning language because of plasticity of the brain.
Ontogenetic	The study of the origin and development of an organism is called ontogenetic.
Sensorimotor	The first of Piaget's stages is the Sensorimotor stage. This stage typically ranges from birth to 2 years. In this stage, children experience the world through their senses. During this stage, object permanence and stranger anxiety develop.
Feedback	Feedback refers to information returned to a person about the effects a response has had.
Phenylketonuria	Phenylketonuria is a genetic disorder in which an individual cannot properly metabolize amino acids. The disorder is now easily detected but, if left untreated, results in mental retardation and hyperactivity.
Hyperactivity	Hyperactivity can be described as a state in which a individual is abnormally easily excitable and exuberant. Strong emotional reactions and a very short span of attention is also typical for the individual.
Seizure	A seizure is a temporary alteration in brain function expressed as a changed mental state, tonic or clonic movements and various other symptoms. They are due to temporary abnormal electrical activity of a group of brain cells.
Tyrosine	Tyrosine is one of the 20 amino acids that are used by cells to synthesize proteins. It plays a key role in signal transduction, since it can be tagged (phosphorylated) with a phosphate group by protein kinases to alter the functionality and activity of certain enzymes.
Enzyme	An enzyme is a protein that catalyzes, or speeds up, a chemical reaction. Enzymes are essential to sustain life because most chemical reactions in biological cells would occur too slowly, or would lead to different products, without enzymes.
Forebrain	The forebrain is the highest level of the brain. Key structures in the forebrain are the limbic system, thalamus, basal ganglia, hypothalamus, and cerebral cortex.
Fraternal twins	Fraternal twins usually occur when two fertilized eggs are implanted in the uterine wall at the same time. The two eggs form two zygotes, and these twins are therefore also known as dizygotic. Dizygotic twins are no more similar genetically than any siblings.
Twin study	A twin study is a kind of genetic study done to determine heritability. The premise is that since identical twins (especially identical twins raised apart) have identical genotypes, differences between them are solely due to environmental factors. By examining the degree to which twins are differentiated, a study may determine the extent to which a particular trait is influenced by genes or the environment.
Infancy	The developmental period that extends from birth to 18 or 24 months is called infancy.
Identical twins	Identical twins occur when a single egg is fertilized to form one zygote (monozygotic) but the zygote then divides into two separate embryos. The two embryos develop into foetuses sharing the same womb. Monozygotic twins are genetically identical unless there has been a mutation in development, and they are almost always the same gender.
Personality	Personality refers to the pattern of enduring characteristics that differentiates a person, the patterns of behaviors that make each individual unique.
Wechsler	Wechsler is best known for his intelligence tests. The Wechsler Adult Intelligence Scale (WAIS) was developed first in 1939 and then called the Wechsler-Bellevue Intelligence Test. From these he derived the Wechsler Intelligence Scale for Children (WISC) in 1949 and the

	Wechsler Preschool and Primary Scale of Intelligence (WPPSI) in 1967. Wechsler originally created these tests to find out more about his patients at the Bellevue clinic and he found the then-current Binet IQ test unsatisfactory.
Wechsler Adult Intelligence Scale	Wechsler adult intelligence scale is an individual intelligence test for adults that yields separate verbal and performance IQ scores as well as an overall IQ score.
Wechsler adult Intelligence	Wechsler adult Intelligence Scale is a revision of the Wechsler-Bellevue test (1939), standardized for use with adults over the age of 16.
Attitude	An enduring mental representation of a person, place, or thing that evokes an emotional response and related behavior is called attitude.
Monozygotic	Identical twins occur when a single egg is fertilized to form one zygote, calld monozygotic, but the zygote then divides into two separate embryos. The two embryos develop into foetuses sharing the same womb. Monozygotic twins are genetically identical unless there has been a mutation in development, and they are almost always the same gender.
Correlation	A statistical technique for determining the degree of association between two or more variables is referred to as correlation.
Intelligence quotient	An intelligence quotient is a score derived from a set of standardized tests that were developed with the purpose of measuring a person's cognitive abilities ("intelligence") in relation to their age group.
Heritability	Heritability It is that proportion of the observed variation in a particular phenotype within a particular population, that can be attributed to the contribution of genotype. In other words: it measures the extent to which differences between individuals in a population are due their being different genetically.
Variability	Statistically, variability refers to how much the scores in a distribution spread out, away from the mean.
Evolutionary perspective	A perspective that focuses on how humans have evolved and adapted behaviors required for survival against various environmental pressures over the long course is called the evolutionary perspective.
Comparative research	Comparative research is a research methodology that aims to make comparisons across different countries or cultures. A major problem is that the data sets in different countries may not use the same categories, or define categories differently.
Depression	In everyday language depression refers to any downturn in mood, which may be relatively transitory and perhaps due to something trivial. This is differentiated from Clinical depression which is marked by symptoms that last two weeks or more and are so severe that they interfere with daily living.
Heredity	Heredity is the transfer of characteristics from parent to offspring through their genes.
Embryo	A developed zygote that has a rudimentary heart, brain, and other organs is referred to as an embryo.

Brain	The brain controls and coordinates most movement, behavior and homeostatic body functions such as heartbeat, blood pressure, fluid balance and body temperature. Functions of the brain are responsible for cognition, emotion, memory, motor learning and other sorts of learning. The brain is primarily made up of two types of cells: glia and neurons.
Nervous system	The body's electrochemical communication circuitry, made up of billions of neurons is a nervous system.
Peripheral nervous system	The peripheral nervous system consists of the nerves and neurons that serve the limbs and organs. It is not protected by bone or the blood-brain barrier, leaving it exposed to toxins and mechanical injuries. The peripheral nervous system is divided into the somatic nervous system and the autonomic nervous system.
Central nervous system	The vertebrate central nervous system consists of the brain and spinal cord.
Spinal cord	The spinal cord is a part of the vertebrate nervous system that is enclosed in and protected by the vertebral column (it passes through the spinal canal). It consists of nerve cells. The spinal cord carries sensory signals and motor innervation to most of the skeletal muscles in the body.
Autonomic nervous system	A division of the peripheral nervous system, the autonomic nervous system, regulates glands and activities such as heartbeat, respiration, digestion, and dilation of the pupils. It is responsible for homeostasis, maintaining a relatively constant internal environment .
Somatic nervous system	The somatic nervous system is the part of the peripheral nervous system associated with the voluntary control of body movements through the action of skeletal muscles. The somatic nervous system consists of afferent fibers which receive information from external sources, and efferent fibers which are responsible for muscle contraction.
Afferent nerve	Axons that carry information inward to the central nervous system from the periphery of the body are called afferent nerve fibers.
Nerve	A nerve is an enclosed, cable-like bundle of nerve fibers or axons, which includes the glia that ensheath the axons in myelin. Neurons are sometimes called nerve cells, though this term is technically imprecise since many neurons do not form nerves.
Efferent nerve	An efferent nerve carries nerve impulses away from the central nervous system. A motor nerve is an efferent nerve involved in muscular control.
Sympathetic	The sympathetic nervous system activates what is often termed the "fight or flight response". It is an automatic regulation system, that is, one that operates without the intervention of conscious thought.
Motor nerve	A motor nerve enables the brain to stimulate muscle contraction. A motor nerve is an efferent nerve that exclusively contains the axons of motorneurons, which innervate skeletal muscle.
Parasympathetic	The parasympathetic nervous system is one of two divisions of the autonomic nervous system. It conserves energy as it slows the heart rate, increases intestinal and gland activity, and relaxes sphincter muscles. In another words, it acts to reverse the effects of the Sympathetic nervous system.
Olfactory nerve	The olfactory nerve is the first of twelve cranial nerves. It consists of a collection of sensory nerve fibers that extend down from the olfactory bulb and pass through the many openings of the cribriform plate, a sieve-like structure. The specialized olfactory receptor neurons of the olfactory nerve are located in the olfactory mucosa of the upper parts of the nasal cavity.
Sensory nerves	Sensory nerves bring impulses toward the central nervous system.

Cranial nerves	Cranial nerves are nerves that emerge from the brainstem instead of the spinal cord. Cranial nerves I and II are named as such, but are technically not nerves, as they are continuations of the central nervous system.
Cranial nerve	A Cranial nerve emerges from the brainstem instead of the spinal cord.
Optic nerve	The optic nerve is the nerve that transmits visual information from the retina to the brain. The optic nerve is composed of retinal ganglion cell axons and support cells.
Vagus nerve	The vagus nerve is tenth of twelve paired cranial nerves and is the only nerve that starts in the brainstem (somewhere in the medulla oblongata) and extends all the way down past the head, right down to the abdomen. The vagus nerve is arguably the single most important nerve in the body.
Neurologist	A physician who studies the nervous system, especially its structure, functions, and abnormalities is referred to as neurologist.
Pathology	Pathology is the study of the processes underlying disease and other forms of illness, harmful abnormality, or dysfunction.
Tumor	A tumor is an abnormal growth that when located in the brain can either be malignant and directly destroy brain tissue, or be benign and disrupt functioning by increasing intracranial pressure.
Meninges	The meninges are the system of membranes that envelop the central nervous system. The meninges consist of three layers, the dura mater, the arachnoid mater, and the pia mater.
Cerebrospinal fluid	A solution that fills the hollow cavities of the brain and circulates around the brain and spinal cord is called cerebrospinal fluid.
Capillary	The capillary is the smallest of a body's blood vessels, measuring 5-10 ìm. They connect arteries and veins, and most closely interact with tissues.
Choroid	The choroid is the vascular layer of the eye lying between the retina and the sclera. The choroid provides oxygen and nourishment to the outer layers of the retina.
Dura mater	The dura mater is the tough and inflexible outermost of the three layers of the meninges surrounding the brain. The other two meninges are the pia mater and the arachnoid mater. The dura mater envelops and protects the brain and spinal cord.
Protein	A protein is a complex, high-molecular-weight organic compound that consists of amino acids joined by peptide bonds. It is essential to the structure and function of all living cells and viruses. Many are enzymes or subunits of enzymes.
Psychoactive drug	A psychoactive drug or psychotropic substance is a chemical that alters brain function, resulting in temporary changes in perception, mood, consciousness, or behavior. Such drugs are often used for recreational and spiritual purposes, as well as in medicine, especially for treating neurological and psychological illnesses.
Glucose	Glucose, a simple monosaccharide sugar, is one of the most important carbohydrates and is used as a source of energy in animals and plants. Glucose is one of the main products of photosynthesis and starts respiration.
Anatomy	Anatomy is the branch of biology that deals with the structure and organization of living things. It can be divided into animal anatomy (zootomy) and plant anatomy (phytonomy). Major branches of anatomy include comparative anatomy, histology, and human anatomy.
Neuron	The neuron is the primary cell of the nervous system. They are found in the brain, the spinal cord, in the nerves and ganglia of the peripheral nervous system. It is a specialized cell that conducts impulses through the nervous system and contains three major parts: cell body, dendrites, and an axon. It can have many dendrites but only one axon.

Membrane protein	A membrane protein is a protein molecule that is attached to, or associated with the membrane of a cell or an organelle. It controls sodium entry: as it depolarizes, sodimum enters.
Learning	Learning is a relatively permanent change in behavior that results from experience. Thus, to attribute a behavioral change to learning, the change must be relatively permanent and must result from experience.
Axon	An axon, or "nerve fiber," is a long slender projection of a nerve cell, or "neuron," which conducts electrical impulses away from the neuron's cell body or soma.
Soma	The soma, or cell body, is the bulbous end of a neuron, containing the nucleus. The cell nucleus is a key feature of the soma. The nucleus is the source of most of the RNA that is produced in neurons and most proteins are produced from mRNAs that do not travel far from the nucleus.
Myelin	Myelin is an electrically insulating fatty layer that surrounds the axons of many neurons, especially those in the peripheral nervous system. The main consequence of a myelin sheath is an increase in the speed at which impulses propagate along the myelinated fiber. The sheath continues to develop throughout childhood.
Nodes of Ranvier	Nodes of Ranvier are regularly spaced gaps in the myelin sheath around an axon or nerve fiber. About one micrometer in length, these gaps expose the membrane of the axon to the surrounding liquid. Ion flow occurs only at the nodes of Ranvier.
Synapse	A synapse is specialized junction through which cells of the nervous system signal to one another and to non-neuronal cells such as muscles or glands.
Ribosome	A ribosome is an organelle composed of rRNA and ribosomal proteins. It translates mRNA into a polypeptide chain (e.g., a protein). It can be thought of as a factory that builds a protein from a set of genetic instructions.
Neurotransmitter	A neurotransmitter is a chemical that is used to relay, amplify and modulate electrical signals between a neurons and another cell.
Cell membrane	A component of every biological cell, the selectively permeable cell membrane is a thin and structured bilayer of phospholipid and protein molecules that envelopes the cell. It separates a cell's interior from its surroundings and controls what moves in and out.
Lipid bilayer	A lipid bilayer is a membrane or zone of a membrane composed of lipid molecules (usually phospholipids). The lipid bilayer is a critical component of all biological membranes, including cell membranes, and is a prerequisite for cell-based organisms.
Projection	Attributing one's own undesirable thoughts, impulses, traits, or behaviors to others is referred to as projection.
Ganglion	A ganglion is a tissue mass that contains the dendrites and cell bodies (or "somas") of nerve cells, in most case ones belonging to the peripheral nervous system. Within the central nervous system such a mass is often called a nucleus.
Nucleus	In neuroanatomy, a cluster of cell bodies of neurons within the central nervous system is a nucleus.
Glial	Glial cells are non-neuronal cells that provide support and nutrition, maintain homeostasis, form myelin, and participate in signal transmission in the nervous system.
Oligodendrocyte	An Oligodendrocyte is a variety of neuroglia. Their main function is the myelination of nerve cells exclusively in the central nervous system of the higher vertebrates. A single oligodendrocyte can extend to about a dozen axons, wrapping around approximately 1mm of each and forming the myelin sheath.
Schwann cell	A Schwann cell is a variety of neuroglia that wraps around axons in the peripheral nervous

	system, forming the myelin sheath. The nervous system depends crucially on this sheath for insulation and an increase in impulse speed.
Myelination	The process in which the nerve cells are covered and insulated with a layer of fat cells, which increases the speed at which information travels through the nervous system is referred to as myelination.
Astrocyte	An astrocyte, also known as astroglia, is a characteristic star-shaped cell in the brain. They are the biggest cells found in brain tissue and outnumber the neurons ten to one. A commonly accepted function is to structure physically the brain. A second function is to provide neurons with nutrients such as glucose. They regulate the flow of nutrients provided by capillaries by forming the blood-brain barrier.
Microglia	Microglia act as the immune cells of the Central nervous system (CNS).
Dendrite	A dendrite is a slender, typically branched projection of a nerve cell, or "neuron," which conducts the electrical stimulation received from other cells to the body or soma of the cell from which it projects. This stimulation arrives through synapses, which typically are located near the tips of the dendrites and away from the soma.
Neuroanatomy	Neuroanatomy is the study of the anatomy of the central nervous system.
Neuroscience	A field that combines the work of psychologists, biologists, biochemists, medical researchers, and others in the study of the structure and function of the nervous system is neuroscience.
Golgi	Golgi discovered a method of staining nervous tissue which would stain a limited number of cells at random, in their entirety. This enabled him to view the paths of nerve cells in the brain for the first time. He called his discovery the black reaction. It is now known universally as the Golgi stain.
Terminal buttons	Terminal buttons are small bulges at the end of axons that send messages to other neurons.
Brain stem	The brain stem is the stalk of the brain below the cerebral hemispheres. It is the major route for communication between the forebrain and the spinal cord and peripheral nerves. It also controls various functions including respiration, regulation of heart rhythms, and primary aspects of sound localization.
Cerebral hemisphere	Either of the two halves that make up the cerebrum is referred to as a cerebral hemisphere. The hemispheres operate together, linked by the corpus callosum, a very large bundle of nerve fibers, and also by other smaller commissures.
Proximal	Students can set both long-term (distal) and short-term (proximal) goals .
White matter	White matter is one of the two main solid components of the central nervous system. It is composed of axons which connect various grey matter areas of the brain to each other and carry nerve impulses between neurons.
Gray matter	Gray matter is a category of nervous tissue with many nerve cell bodies and few myelinated axons. Generally, gray matter can be understood as the parts of the brain responsible for information processing; whereas, white matter is responsible for information transmission. In addition, gray matter does not have a myelin sheath and does not regenerate after injury unlike white matter.
Interneurons	Interneurons are the neurons that provide connections between sensory and motor neurons, as well as between themselves.
Interneuron	An interneuron (also called relay neuron or association neuron) is a neuron that communicates only to other neurons.
Spinal nerve	The term spinal nerve generally refers to the mixed spinal nerve, which is formed from the

	dorsal and ventral roots that come out of the spinal cord. The spinal nerve passes out of the vertebrae through the intervertebral foramen.
Sensory neuron	A sensory neuron is an afferent nerve cell within the nervous system responsible for converting external stimuli from the organism's environment into internal electrical impulses. It carries messages from a sensory organ, through a nerve, into the brain or spinal cord.
Motor neuron	A motor neuron is an efferent neuron that originates in the spinal cord and synapses with muscle fibers to facilitate muscle contraction and with muscle spindles to modify proprioceptive sensitivity.
Embryo	A developed zygote that has a rudimentary heart, brain, and other organs is referred to as an embryo.
Neural tube	The neural tube is the embryonal structure that gives rise to the brain and spinal cord.
Forebrain	The forebrain is the highest level of the brain. Key structures in the forebrain are the limbic system, thalamus, basal ganglia, hypothalamus, and cerebral cortex.
Hindbrain	The lowest level of the brain, consisting of the medulla, cerebellum, and pons is called the hindbrain.
Mesencephalon	The mesencephalon is archipallian in origin, meaning its general architecture is shared with the most ancient of vertebrates. Dopamine produced in the subtantia nigra plays a role in motivation and habituation of species from humans to the most elementary animals such as insects.
Diencephalon	The diencephalon is the region of the brain that includes the epithalamus, thalamus, and hypothalamus. It is located above the mesencephalon of the brain stem. Sensory information is relayed between the brain stem and the rest of the brain regions
Midbrain	Located between the hindbrain and forebrain, a region in which many nerve-fiber systems ascend and descend to connect the higher and lower portions of the brain is referred to as midbrain. It is archipallian in origin, meaning its general architecture is shared with the most ancient of vertebrates. Dopamine produced in the subtantia nigra plays a role in motivation and habituation of species from humans to the most elementary animals such as insects.
Reticular formation	Reticular formation is a part of the brain which is involved in stereotypical actions, such as walking, sleeping, and lying down. The reticular formation, phylogenetically one of the oldest portions of the brain, is a poorly-differentiated area of the brain stem.
Arousal	Arousal is a physiological and psychological state involving the activation of the reticular activating system in the brain stem, the autonomic nervous system and the endocrine system, leading to increased heart rate and blood pressure and a condition of alertness and readiness to respond.
Reticular activating system	The reticular activating system is the part of the brain believed to be the center of arousal and motivation. It is situated between the brain stem and the central nervous system (CNS).
Cerebellum	The cerebellum is located in the inferior posterior portion of the head (the hindbrain), directly dorsal to the brainstem and pons, inferior to the occipital lobe. The cerebellum is a region of the brain that plays an important role in the integration of sensory perception and fine motor output.
Pons	The pons is a knob on the brain stem. It is part of the autonomic nervous system, and relays sensory information between the cerebellum and cerebrum. Some theories posit that it has a role in dreaming.

Sensorimotor	The first of Piaget's stages is the Sensorimotor stage. This stage typically ranges from birth to 2 years. In this stage, children experience the world through their senses. During this stage, object permanence and stranger anxiety develop.
Substantia nigra	The substantia nigra is a portion of the midbrain thought to be involved in certain aspects of movement and attention. Degeneration of cells in this region is the principle pathology that underlies Parkinson's disease.
Hypothalamus	The hypothalamus is a region of the brain located below the thalamus, forming the major portion of the ventral region of the diencephalon and functioning to regulate certain metabolic processes and other autonomic activities.
Thalamus	An area near the center of the brain involved in the relay of sensory information to the cortex and in the functions of sleep and attention is the thalamus.
Lobes	The four major sections of the cerebral cortex: frontal, parietal, temporal, and occipital are called lobes.
Receptor	A sensory receptor is a structure that recognizes a stimulus in the internal or external environment of an organism. In response to stimuli the sensory receptor initiates sensory transduction by creating graded potentials or action potentials in the same cell or in an adjacent one.
Sensory receptor	A sensory receptor is a structure that recognizes a stimulus in the environment of an organism. In response to stimuli the sensory receptor initiates sensory transduction by creating graded potentials or action potentials in the same cell or in an adjacent one.
Pituitary gland	The pituitary gland is an endocrine gland about the size of a pea that sits in the small, bony cavity at the base of the brain. The pituitary gland secretes hormones regulating a wide variety of bodily activities, including trophic hormones that stimulate other endocrine glands.
Hormone	A hormone is a chemical messenger from one cell (or group of cells) to another. The best known are those produced by endocrine glands, but they are produced by nearly every organ system. The function of hormones is to serve as a signal to the target cells; the action of the hormone is determined by the pattern of secretion and the signal transduction of the receiving tissue.
Gland	A gland is an organ in an animal's body that synthesizes a substance for release such as hormones, often into the bloodstream or into cavities inside the body or its outer surface.
Mammillary body	The mammillary body is a pair of small round bodies in the brain forming part of the limbic system. Symptoms from damage to the mammillary bodies can include impaired memory, also called anterograde amnesia; this suggests that the mammillary bodies might be important for memory.
Optic chiasm	Optic chiasm refers to the point at which the optic nerves from the inside half of each eye cross over and then project to the opposite half of the brain.
Problem solving	An attempt to find an appropriate way of attaining a goal when the goal is not readily available is called problem solving.
Species	Species refers to a reproductively isolated breeding population.
Sulcus	A sulcus is a depression or fissure in the surface of an organ, most especially the brain. In the brain it surrounds the gyri, creating the characteristic appearance of the brain.
Gyrus	A gyrus is a ridge on the cerebral cortex. It is generally surrounded by one or more sulci.
Longitudinal fissure	The longitudinal fissure is the fissure (groove) that runs from the rostral to caudal portion of the brain, that serves to separate the left and right hemispheres

Evolution	Commonly used to refer to gradual change, evolution is the change in the frequency of alleles within a population from one generation to the next. This change may be caused by different mechanisms, including natural selection, genetic drift, or changes in population (gene flow).
Neocortex	The neocortex is part of the cerebral cortex which covers most of the surface of the cerebral hemispheres including the frontal, parietal, occipital, and temporal lobes. Often seen as the hallmark of human intelligence, the role of this structure in the brain appears to be involved in conscious thought, spatial reasoning, and sensory perception.
Cerebral cortex	The cerebral cortex is the outermost layer of the cerebrum and has a grey color. It is made up of four lobes and it is involved in many complex brain functions including memory, perceptual awareness, "thinking", language and consciousness. The cerebral cortex receives sensory information from many different sensory organs eg: eyes, ears, etc. and processes the information.
Hippocampus	The hippocampus is a part of the brain located inside the temporal lobe. It forms a part of the limbic system and plays a part in memory and navigation.
Temporal lobe	The temporal lobe is part of the cerebrum. It lies at the side of the brain, beneath the lateral or Sylvian fissure. Adjacent areas in the superior, posterior and lateral parts of the temporal lobe are involved in high-level auditory processing.
Basal ganglia	The basal ganglia are a group of nuclei in the brain associated with motor and learning functions.
Limbic system	The limbic system is a group of brain structures that are involved in various emotions such as aggression, fear, pleasure and also in the formation of memory. The limbic system affects the endocrine system and the autonomic nervous system. It consists of several subcortical structures located around the thalamus.
Lateral fissure	The lateral fissure is one of the most prominent structures of the human brain. It divides the frontal lobe and parietal lobe above from the temporal lobe below.
Motivation	In psychology, motivation is the driving force (desire) behind all actions of an organism.
Amygdala	Located in the brain's medial temporal lobe, the almond-shaped amygdala is believed to play a key role in the emotions. It forms part of the limbic system and is linked to both fear responses and pleasure. Its size is positively correlated with aggressive behavior across species.
Cingulate cortex	The part of the limbic system that is believed to process cognitive information in emotion is the cingulate cortex. The cingulate cortex is part of the brain and situated roughly in the middle of the cortex.
Cingulate gyrus	Cingulate gyrus is a gyrus in the medial part of the brain. It partially wraps around the corpus callosum and is limited above by the cingulate sulcus. It functions as an intergral part of the limbic system, which is involved with emotion formation and processing, learning, and memory.
Corpus callosum	The corpus callosum is the largest white matter structure in the brain. It consists of mostly of contralateral axon projections. The corpus callosum connects the left and right cerebral hemispheres. Most communication between regions in different halves of the brain are carried over the corpus callosum.
Tremor	Tremor is the rhythmic, oscillating shaking movement of the whole body or just a certain part of it, caused by problems of the neurons responsible from muscle action.
Parietal lobe	The parietal lobe is positioned above (superior to) the occipital lobe and behind (posterior to) the frontal lobe. It plays important roles in integrating sensory information from various senses, and in the manipulation of objects.

Frontal lobe

The frontal lobe comprises four major folds of cortical tissue: the precentral gyrus, superior gyrus and the middle gyrus of the frontal gyri, the inferior frontal gyrus. It has been found to play a part in impulse control, judgement, language, memory, motor function, problem solving, sexual behavior, socialization and spontaneity.

Superior temporal gyrus

The superior temporal gyrus is one of three gyri in the temporal lobe of the human brain. The superior temporal gyrus contains several important structures of the brain, including: -- Brodmann areas, marking the location of the primary auditory cortex; Wernicke's area, an important region for the processing of speech so that it can be understood as language.

Olds and Milner

Olds and Milner discovered that electrical stimulation of a particular region in the Mesolimbic dopamine system was highly rewarding to rats; at first believed they had discovered "the pleasure centre" in the brain; it now appears that stimulation of many regions of the mesolimbic system can lead to rewarding effects--the key is that dopamine ultimately reaches neurons in the nucleus accumbens, a limbic system structure.

Biopsychology

Biopsychology is the scientific study of the biological bases of behavior and mental states. Empirical experiments study changes in central nervous system activation in response to a stimulus.

Electrode

Any device used to electrically stimulate nerve tissue or to record its activity is an electrode.

Anatomy	Anatomy is the branch of biology that deals with the structure and organization of living things. It can be divided into animal anatomy (zootomy) and plant anatomy (phytonomy). Major branches of anatomy include comparative anatomy, histology, and human anatomy.
Neuron	The neuron is the primary cell of the nervous system. They are found in the brain, the spinal cord, in the nerves and ganglia of the peripheral nervous system. It is a specialized cell that conducts impulses through the nervous system and contains three major parts: cell body, dendrites, and an axon. It can have many dendrites but only one axon.
Synapse	A synapse is specialized junction through which cells of the nervous system signal to one another and to non-neuronal cells such as muscles or glands.
Biopsychology	Biopsychology is the scientific study of the biological bases of behavior and mental states. Empirical experiments study changes in central nervous system activation in response to a stimulus.
Case study	A carefully drawn biography that may be obtained through interviews, questionnaires, and psychological tests is called a case study.
Electrode	Any device used to electrically stimulate nerve tissue or to record its activity is an electrode.
Nerve	A nerve is an enclosed, cable-like bundle of nerve fibers or axons, which includes the glia that ensheath the axons in myelin. Neurons are sometimes called nerve cells, though this term is technically imprecise since many neurons do not form nerves.
Substantia nigra	The substantia nigra is a portion of the midbrain thought to be involved in certain aspects of movement and attention. Degeneration of cells in this region is the principle pathology that underlies Parkinson's disease.
Dopamine	Dopamine is critical to the way the brain controls our movements and is a crucial part of the basal ganglia motor loop. It is commonly associated with the 'pleasure system' of the brain, providing feelings of enjoyment and reinforcement to motivate us to do, or continue doing, certain activities.
Neurologist	A physician who studies the nervous system, especially its structure, functions, and abnormalities is referred to as neurologist.
Biopsychologist	A psychologist who studies the relationship between behavior and biological processes, especially activity in the nervous system is referred to as a Biopsychologist.
Microelectrode	An electrical wire so small that it can be used either to monitor the electrical activity of a single neuron or to stimulate activity within it is a microelectrode.
Resting state	Resting state is a negative electrical charge of about 270 millivolts within a neuron.
Ion	An ion is an atom or group of atoms with a net electric charge. The energy required to detach an electron in its lowest energy state from an atom or molecule of a gas with less net electric charge is called the ionization potential, or ionization energy.
Resting potential	The resting potential of a cell is the membrane potential that would be maintained if there were no action potentials, synaptic potentials, or other active changes in the membrane potential. In most cells the resting potential has a negative value, which by convention means that there is excess negative charge inside compared to outside.
Nervous system	The body's electrochemical communication circuitry, made up of billions of neurons is a nervous system.
Concentration gradient	An ion gradient is a concentration gradient of ions, it can be called an electrochemical potential gradient of ions across membranes.

Protein	A protein is a complex, high-molecular-weight organic compound that consists of amino acids joined by peptide bonds. It is essential to the structure and function of all living cells and viruses. Many are enzymes or subunits of enzymes.
Ion channel	An Ion channel is a pore-forming protein that help establish the small voltage gradient that exists across the membrane of all living cells, by controlling the flow of ions. They are present in the membranes that surround all biological cells.
Cell membrane	A component of every biological cell, the selectively permeable cell membrane is a thin and structured bilayer of phospholipid and protein molecules that envelopes the cell. It separates a cell's interior from its surroundings and controls what moves in and out.
Postsynaptic Potential	A postsynaptic potential is a function of two neurons synapsing, whereby Neuron A causes a change in Neuron B's membrane potential.
Synaptic cleft	Synaptic cleft refers to a microscopic gap between the terminal button of a neuron and the cell membrane of another neuron.
Receptor	A sensory receptor is a structure that recognizes a stimulus in the internal or external environment of an organism. In response to stimuli the sensory receptor initiates sensory transduction by creating graded potentials or action potentials in the same cell or in an adjacent one.
Neurotransmitter	A neurotransmitter is a chemical that is used to relay, amplify and modulate electrical signals between a neurons and another cell.
Inhibitory postsynaptic potential	Inhibitory postsynaptic potential refers to a local, graded excitatory potential that hyperpolarizes a neuron's membrane--driving the charge farther negative. Driving a cell to negativity will usually lower the firing rate.
Hyperpolariz-tion	Hyperpolarization is any change in a cell's membrane potential that makes it more polarized. That is, hyperpolarization is an increase in the absolute value of a cell's membrane potential.
Dendrite	A dendrite is a slender, typically branched projection of a nerve cell, or "neuron," which conducts the electrical stimulation received from other cells to the body or soma of the cell from which it projects. This stimulation arrives through synapses, which typically are located near the tips of the dendrites and away from the soma.
Action potential	The electrical impulse that provides the basis for the conduction of a neural impulse along an axon of a neuron is the action potential. When a biological cell or patch of membrane undergoes an action potential, or electrical excitation, the polarity of the transmembrane voltage swings rapidly from negative to positive and back.
Axon	An axon, or "nerve fiber," is a long slender projection of a nerve cell, or "neuron," which conducts electrical impulses away from the neuron's cell body or soma.
Axon hillock	The axon hillock is the anatomical part of a neuron that connects the cell body to the axon. It is regarded as the place where EPSPs from numerous synaptic inputs on the dendrites or cell body accumulate.
Inhibitory synapse	An inhibitory synapse is a synapse in which an action potential in the presynaptic cell decreases the probability of an action potential occurring in the postsynaptic cell.
Amplitude	Amplitude is a nonnegative scalar measure of a wave's magnitude of oscillation.
Threshold	In general, a threshold is a fixed location or value where an abrupt change is observed. In the sensory modalities, it is the minimum amount of stimulus energy necessary to elicit a sensory response.
Temporal	Temporal summation is combining the effects of a single or a small number of EPSPs that occur

summation	rapidly within a short time at the same synapse until they reach the action potential of the cell.
Potassium channel	The potassium channel is the most common type of ion channel. They are found in most cells, and control the electrical excitability of the cell membrane. In neurons, they shape action potentials and set the resting membrane potential. They regulate cellular processes such as the secretion of hormones, so their malfunction can lead to diseases.
Refractory period	Refractory period refers to a phase following firing during which a neuron is less sensitive to messages from other neurons and will not fire. In the sexual response cycle, it is a period of time following orgasm during which an individual is not responsive to sexual stimulation.
Relative refractory period	Relative refractory period is a period of time where the stimulus must exceed the usual threshold to produce action potential.
Absolute refractory period	The refractory period in a neuron occurs after an action potential. The action potential ends when voltage-gated ion channels allow positively charged potassium ions to leave the cell, between the 2nd and 3rd millisecond after the action potential. During this repolarization period when the potassium ion-channels are open, it is impossible to have another action potential. As a result, this is known as the absolute refractory period.
Baseline	Measure of a particular behavior or process taken before the introduction of the independent variable or treatment is called the baseline.
Analogy	An analogy is a comparison between two different things, in order to highlight some form of similarity. Analogy is the cognitive process of transferring information from a particular subject to another particular subject.
Terminal buttons	Terminal buttons are small bulges at the end of axons that send messages to other neurons.
Myelin	Myelin is an electrically insulating fatty layer that surrounds the axons of many neurons, especially those in the peripheral nervous system. The main consequence of a myelin sheath is an increase in the speed at which impulses propagate along the myelinated fiber. The sheath continues to develop throughout childhood.
Nodes of Ranvier	Nodes of Ranvier are regularly spaced gaps in the myelin sheath around an axon or nerve fiber. About one micrometer in length, these gaps expose the membrane of the axon to the surrounding liquid. Ion flow occurs only at the nodes of Ranvier.
Myelination	The process in which the nerve cells are covered and insulated with a layer of fat cells, which increases the speed at which information travels through the nervous system is referred to as myelination.
Skeletal muscle	Skeletal muscle is a type of striated muscle, attached to the skeleton. They are used to facilitate movement, by applying force to bones and joints; via contraction. They generally contract voluntarily (via nerve stimulation), although they can contract involuntarily.
Motor neuron	A motor neuron is an efferent neuron that originates in the spinal cord and synapses with muscle fibers to facilitate muscle contraction and with muscle spindles to modify proprioceptive sensitivity.
Dendritic spine	A dendritic spine is a small membranous extrusion that protrudes from a dendrite and forms one half of a synapse. Changes in dendritic spine density underlie many brain functions, including motivation, learning, and memory. In particular, long-term memory is mediated in part by the growth of new dendritic spines to reinforce a particular neural pathway.
Peptides	Peptides are the family of molecules formed from the linking, in a defined order, of various amino acids.

Golgi	Golgi discovered a method of staining nervous tissue which would stain a limited number of cells at random, in their entirety. This enabled him to view the paths of nerve cells in the brain for the first time. He called his discovery the black reaction. It is now known universally as the Golgi stain.
Amino acid	Amino acid is the basic structural building unit of proteins. They form short polymer chains called peptides or polypeptides which in turn form structures called proteins.
Cytoplasm	Cytoplasm is the colloidal, semi-fluid matter contained within the cell's plasma membrane, in which organelles are suspended. In contrast to the protoplasm, the cytoplasm does not include the cell nucleus, the interior of which is made up of nucleoplasm.
Ribosome	A ribosome is an organelle composed of rRNA and ribosomal proteins. It translates mRNA into a polypeptide chain (e.g., a protein). It can be thought of as a factory that builds a protein from a set of genetic instructions.
Brain	The brain controls and coordinates most movement, behavior and homeostatic body functions such as heartbeat, blood pressure, fluid balance and body temperature. Functions of the brain are responsible for cognition, emotion, memory, motor learning and other sorts of learning. The brain is primarily made up of two types of cells: glia and neurons.
Stages	Stages represent relatively discrete periods of time in which functioning is qualitatively different from functioning at other periods.
Reuptake	Reuptake is the reabsorption of a neurotransmitter by the molecular transporter of a pre-synaptic neuron after it has performed its function of transmitting a neural impulse.
Astrocyte	An astrocyte, also known as astroglia, is a characteristic star-shaped cell in the brain. They are the biggest cells found in brain tissue and outnumber the neurons ten to one. A commonly accepted function is to structure physically the brain. A second function is to provide neurons with nutrients such as glucose. They regulate the flow of nutrients provided by capillaries by forming the blood-brain barrier.
Glial	Glial cells are non-neuronal cells that provide support and nutrition, maintain homeostasis, form myelin, and participate in signal transmission in the nervous system.
Enzyme	An enzyme is a protein that catalyzes, or speeds up, a chemical reaction. Enzymes are essential to sustain life because most chemical reactions in biological cells would occur too slowly, or would lead to different products, without enzymes.
Neuropeptides	Brain chemicals, such as enkephalins and endorphins, that regulate the activity of neurons are called neuropeptides.
Central nervous system	The vertebrate central nervous system consists of the brain and spinal cord.
Glutamate	Glutamate is one of the 20 standard amino acids used by all organisms in their proteins. It is critical for proper cell function, but it is not an essential nutrient in humans because it can be manufactured from other compounds.
Brain stem	The brain stem is the stalk of the brain below the cerebral hemispheres. It is the major route for communication between the forebrain and the spinal cord and peripheral nerves. It also controls various functions including respiration, regulation of heart rhythms, and primary aspects of sound localization.
Epinephrine	Epinephrine is a hormone and a neurotransmitter. Epinephrine plays a central role in the short-term stress reaction—the physiological response to threatening or exciting conditions. It is secreted by the adrenal medulla. When released into the bloodstream, epinephrine binds to multiple receptors and has numerous effects throughout the body.

Norepinephrine	Norepinephrine is released from the adrenal glands as a hormone into the blood, but it is also a neurotransmitter in the nervous system. As a stress hormone, it affects parts of the human brain where attention and impulsivity are controlled. Along with epinephrine, this compound effects the fight-or-flight response, activating the sympathetic nervous system to directly increase heart rate, release energy from fat, and increase muscle readiness.
Catecholamines	Catecholamines are chemical compounds derived from the amino acid tyrosine that act as hormones or neurotransmitters. High catecholamine levels in blood are associated with stress.
Tyrosine	Tyrosine is one of the 20 amino acids that are used by cells to synthesize proteins. It plays a key role in signal transduction, since it can be tagged (phosphorylated) with a phosphate group by protein kinases to alter the functionality and activity of certain enzymes.
Tryptophan	Tryptophan is a sleep-promoting amino acid and a precursor for serotonin (a neurotransmitter) and melatonin (a neurohormone). Tryptophan has been implicated as a possible cause of schizophrenia in people who cannot metabolize it properly.
Serotonin	Serotonin, a neurotransmitter, is believed to play an important part of the biochemistry of depression, bipolar disorder and anxiety. It is also believed to be influential on sexuality and appetite.
Noradrenaline	Noradrenaline is released from the adrenal glands as a hormone into the blood, but it is also a neurotransmitter in the nervous system. As a stress hormone, it affects parts of the human brain where attention and impulsivity are controlled. Along with epinephrine, this compound effects the fight-or-flight response, activating the sympathetic nervous system to directly increase heart rate, release energy from fat, and increase muscle readiness.
Adrenaline	Adrenaline refers to a hormone produced by the adrenal medulla that stimulates sympathetic ANS activity and generally arouses people and heightens their emotional responsiveness.
Feedback	Feedback refers to information returned to a person about the effects a response has had.
Acetylcholine	The chemical compound acetylcholine was the first neurotransmitter to be identified. It plays a role in learning, memory, and rapid eye movement sleep and causes the skeletal muscle fibers to contract.
Autonomic nervous system	A division of the peripheral nervous system, the autonomic nervous system, regulates glands and activities such as heartbeat, respiration, digestion, and dilation of the pupils. It is responsible for homeostasis, maintaining a relatively constant internal environment .
Endorphin	An endorphin is an endogenous opioid biochemical compound. They are peptides produced by the pituitary gland and the hypothalamus, and they resemble the opiates in their abilities to produce analgesia and a sense of well-being. In other words, they work as "natural pain killers."
Morphine	Morphine, the principal active agent in opium, is a powerful opioid analgesic drug. According to recent research, it may also be produced naturally by the human brain. Morphine is usually highly addictive, and tolerance and physical and psychological dependence develop quickly.
Opiates	A group of narcotics derived from the opium poppy that provide a euphoric rush and depress the nervous system are referred to as opiates.
Heroin	Heroin is widely and illegally used as a powerful and addictive drug producing intense euphoria, which often disappears with increasing tolerance. Heroin is a semi-synthetic opioid. It is the 3,6-diacetyl derivative of morphine and is synthesised from it by acetylation.
Opium	Opium is a narcotic analgesic drug which is obtained from the unripe seed pods of the opium poppy. Regular use, even for a few days, invariably leads to physical tolerance and dependence. Various degrees of psychological addiction can occur, though this is relatively

	rare when opioids are properly used..
Analgesia	Analgesia refers to insensitivity to pain without loss of consciousness.
Agonist	Agonist refers to a drug that mimics or increases a neurotransmitter's effects.
Cocaine	Cocaine is a crystalline tropane alkaloid that is obtained from the leaves of the coca plant. It is a stimulant of the central nervous system and an appetite suppressant, creating what has been described as a euphoric sense of happiness and increased energy.
Blocking	If the one of the two members of a compound stimulus fails to produce the CR due to an earlier conditioning of the other member of the compound stimulus, blocking has occurred.
Diazepam	Diazepam, brand names: Valium, Seduxen, in Europe Apozepam, Diapam, is a 1,4-benzodiazepine derivative, which possesses anxiolytic, anticonvulsant, sedative and skeletal muscle relaxant properties. Diazepam is used to treat anxiety and tension, and is the most effective benzodiazepine for treating muscle spasms.
Benzodiazepines	The benzodiazepines are a class of drugs with hypnotic, anxiolytic, anticonvulsant, amnestic and muscle relaxant properties. Benzodiazepines are often used for short-term relief of severe, disabling anxiety or insomnia.
Sedative	A sedative is a drug that depresses the central nervous system (CNS), which causes calmness, relaxation, reduction of anxiety, sleepiness, slowed breathing, slurred speech, staggering gait, poor judgment, and slow, uncertain reflexes.
Anxiety	Anxiety is a complex combination of the feeling of fear, apprehension and worry often accompanied by physical sensations such as palpitations, chest pain and/or shortness of breath.
Hippocrates	Hippocrates was an ancient Greek physician, commonly regarded as one of the most outstanding figures in medicine of all time; he has been called "the father of medicine."
Belladonna	Deadly nightshade or belladonna is a well-known, hardy perennial shrub, a member of the nightshade family. It is one of the most toxic plants to be found in the Western hemisphere. Children have been poisoned by as few as three of the berries, and a small leaf thoroughly chewed can be a fatal dose for an adult.
Pupil	In the eye, the pupil is the opening in the middle of the iris. It appears black because most of the light entering it is absorbed by the tissues inside the eye. The size of the pupil is controlled by involuntary contraction and dilation of the iris, in order to regulate the intensity of light entering the eye. This is known as the pupillary reflex.
Curare	Curare is a drug that once entered into the bloodstream and reaches the muscles it blocks the receptors on the muscles, paralyzing the muscles.
Nicotine	Nicotine is an organic compound, an alkaloid found naturally throughout the tobacco plant, with a high concentration in the leaves. It is a potent nerve poison and is included in many insecticides. In lower concentrations, the substance is a stimulant and is one of the main factors leading to the pleasure and habit-forming qualities of tobacco smoking.
Evolutionary perspective	A perspective that focuses on how humans have evolved and adapted behaviors required for survival against various environmental pressures over the long course is called the evolutionary perspective.
Metaphor	A metaphor is a rhetorical trope where a comparison is made between two seemingly unrelated subjects
Gene	A gene is an ultramicroscopic area of the chromosome. It is the smallest physical unit of the DNA molecule that carries a piece of hereditary information.

Brain	The brain controls and coordinates most movement, behavior and homeostatic body functions such as heartbeat, blood pressure, fluid balance and body temperature. Functions of the brain are responsible for cognition, emotion, memory, motor learning and other sorts of learning. The brain is primarily made up of two types of cells: glia and neurons.
Nerve	A nerve is an enclosed, cable-like bundle of nerve fibers or axons, which includes the glia that ensheath the axons in myelin. Neurons are sometimes called nerve cells, though this term is technically imprecise since many neurons do not form nerves.
Somatosensory	Somatosensory system consists of the various sensory receptors that trigger the experiences labelled as touch or pressure, temperature, pain, and the sensations of muscle movement and joint position including posture, movement, and facial expression.
Somatosensory cortex	The primary somatosensory cortex is across the central sulcus and behind the primary motor cortex configured to generally correspond with the arrangement of nearby motor cells related to specific body parts. It is the main sensory receptive area for the sense of touch.
Cranial nerve	A Cranial nerve emerges from the brainstem instead of the spinal cord.
Tumor	A tumor is an abnormal growth that when located in the brain can either be malignant and directly destroy brain tissue, or be benign and disrupt functioning by increasing intracranial pressure.
Biopsychologist	A psychologist who studies the relationship between behavior and biological processes, especially activity in the nervous system is referred to as a Biopsychologist.
Research method	The scope of the research method is to produce some new knowledge. This, in principle, can take three main forms: Exploratory research; Constructive research; and Empirical research.
Biopsychology	Biopsychology is the scientific study of the biological bases of behavior and mental states. Empirical experiments study changes in central nervous system activation in response to a stimulus.
Displacement	An unconscious defense mechanism in which the individual directs aggressive or sexual feelings away from the primary object to someone or something safe is referred to as displacement. Displacement in linguistics is simply the ability to talk about things not present.
Computed tomography	Computed tomography is an imaging method employing tomography where digital processing is used to generate a three-dimensional image of the internals of an object from a large series of two-dimensional X-ray images taken around a single axis of rotation.
Magnetic resonance imaging	Magnetic resonance imaging is a method of creating images of the inside of opaque organs in living organisms as well as detecting the amount of bound water in geological structures. It is primarily used to demonstrate pathological or other physiological alterations of living tissues and is a commonly used form of medical imaging.
MRI scan	An MRI scan is a method of creating images of the inside of opaque organs in living organisms as well as detecting the amount of bound water in geological structures. It is primarily used to demonstrate pathological or other physiological alterations of living tissues and is a commonly used form of medical imaging.
Positron emission tomography	Positron Emission Tomography measures emissions from radioactively labeled chemicals that have been injected into the bloodstream. The greatest benefit is that different compounds can show blood flow and oxygen and glucose metabolism in the tissues of the working brain.
Glucose	Glucose, a simple monosaccharide sugar, is one of the most important carbohydrates and is used as a source of energy in animals and plants. Glucose is one of the main products of photosynthesis and starts respiration.

Neuron — The neuron is the primary cell of the nervous system. They are found in the brain, the spinal cord, in the nerves and ganglia of the peripheral nervous system. It is a specialized cell that conducts impulses through the nervous system and contains three major parts: cell body, dendrites, and an axon. It can have many dendrites but only one axon.

Pet scan — PET Scan measures emissions from radioactively labeled chemicals that have been injected into the bloodstream. The greatest benefit is that different compounds can show blood flow and oxygen and glucose metabolism in the tissues of the working brain.

Coding — In senation, coding is the process by which information about the quality and quantity of a stimulus is preserved in the pattern of action potentials sent through sensory neurons to the central nervous system.

Cognition — The intellectual processes through which information is obtained, transformed, stored, retrieved, and otherwise used is cognition.

Electrode — Any device used to electrically stimulate nerve tissue or to record its activity is an electrode.

Electroencep-alography — Electroencephalography is the neurophysiologic measurement of the electrical activity of the brain by recording from electrodes placed on the scalp, or in special cases on the cortex. The resulting traces are known as an electroencephalogram (EEG) and represent so-called brainwaves.

Consciousness — The awareness of the sensations, thoughts, and feelings being experienced at a given moment is called consciousness.

Alpha wave — The brain wave associated with deep relaxation is referred to as the alpha wave. Recorded by electroencephalography (EEG) , they are synchronous and coherent (regular like sawtooth) and in the frequency range of 8 - 12 Hz. It is also called Berger's wave in memory of the founder of EEG.

Pathology — Pathology is the study of the processes underlying disease and other forms of illness, harmful abnormality, or dysfunction.

Epilepsy — Epilepsy is a chronic neurological condition characterized by recurrent unprovoked neural discharges. It is commonly controlled with medication, although surgical methods are used as well.

Deep sleep — Deep sleep refers to stage 4 sleep; the deepest form of normal sleep.

Electroencep-alogram — Electroencephalography is the neurophysiologic measurement of the electrical activity of the brain by recording from electrodes placed on the scalp, or in the special cases on the cortex. The resulting traces are known as an electroencephalogram and represent so-called brainwaves.

Neuroscience — A field that combines the work of psychologists, biologists, biochemists, medical researchers, and others in the study of the structure and function of the nervous system is neuroscience.

Stimulus — A change in an environmental condition that elicits a response is a stimulus.

Latency — In child development, latency refers to a phase of psychosexual development characterized by repression of sexual impulses. In learning theory, latency is the delay between stimulus (S) and response (R), which according to Hull depends on the strength of the association.

Amplitude — Amplitude is a nonnegative scalar measure of a wave's magnitude of oscillation.

Theta wave — A theta wave is an electroencephalogram pattern normally produced while awake but relaxed or drowsy. The pattern has a frequency of 3.5 to 7.5 Hz. They are strong during internal focus, meditation, prayer, and spiritual awareness.

Cingulate cortex	The part of the limbic system that is believed to process cognitive information in emotion is the cingulate cortex. The cingulate cortex is part of the brain and situated roughly in the middle of the cortex.
Skeletal muscle	Skeletal muscle is a type of striated muscle, attached to the skeleton. They are used to facilitate movement, by applying force to bones and joints; via contraction. They generally contract voluntarily (via nerve stimulation), although they can contract involuntarily.
Motor neuron	A motor neuron is an efferent neuron that originates in the spinal cord and synapses with muscle fibers to facilitate muscle contraction and with muscle spindles to modify proprioceptive sensitivity.
Electromyography	Electromyography is a medical technique for measuring muscle response to nervous stimulation.
Emotion	An emotion is a mental states that arise spontaneously, rather than through conscious effort. They are often accompanied by physiological changes.
Gland	A gland is an organ in an animal's body that synthesizes a substance for release such as hormones, often into the bloodstream or into cavities inside the body or its outer surface.
Cardiovascular system	The human cardiovascular system comprises the blood, the heart, and a dual-circuit system of blood vessels that serve as conduits between the heart, the lungs, and the peripheral tissues of the body.
Electrocardi-gram	An electrocardiogram is a graphic produced by an electrocardiograph, which records the electrical voltage in the heart in the form of a continuous strip graph. It is the prime tool in cardiac electrophysiology, and has a prime function in screening and diagnosis of cardiovascular diseases..
Mercury	Elemental, liquid mercury is slightly toxic, while its vapor, compounds and salts are highly toxic and have been implicated as causing brain and liver damage when ingested, inhaled or contacted. Because mercury is easily transferred across the placenta, the embryo is highly susceptible to birth defects.
Diastolic blood pressure	Blood pressure level when the heart is at rest or between heartbeats is called diastolic blood pressure.
Hypertension	Hypertension is a medical condition where the blood pressure in the arteries is chronically elevated. Persistent hypertension is one of the risk factors for strokes, heart attacks, heart failure and arterial aneurysm, and is a leading cause of chronic renal failure.
Chronic	Chronic refers to a relatively long duration, usually more than a few months.
Genitals	Genitals refers to the internal and external reproductive organs.
Arousal	Arousal is a physiological and psychological state involving the activation of the reticular activating system in the brain stem, the autonomic nervous system and the endocrine system, leading to increased heart rate and blood pressure and a condition of alertness and readiness to respond.
Lesion	A lesion is a non-specific term referring to abnormal tissue in the body. It can be caused by any disease process including trauma (physical, chemical, electrical), infection, neoplasm, metabolic and autoimmune.
Amygdala	Located in the brain's medial temporal lobe, the almond-shaped amygdala is believed to play a key role in the emotions. It forms part of the limbic system and is linked to both fear responses and pleasure. Its size is positively correlated with aggressive behavior across species.
White matter	White matter is one of the two main solid components of the central nervous system. It is composed of axons which connect various grey matter areas of the brain to each other and

	carry nerve impulses between neurons.
Species	Species refers to a reproductively isolated breeding population.
Microelectrode	An electrical wire so small that it can be used either to monitor the electrical activity of a single neuron or to stimulate activity within it is a microelectrode.
Action potential	The electrical impulse that provides the basis for the conduction of a neural impulse along an axon of a neuron is the action potential. When a biological cell or patch of membrane undergoes an action potential, or electrical excitation, the polarity of the transmembrane voltage swings rapidly from negative to positive and back.
Psychopharma-ology	Psychopharmacology refers to the study of the effects of drugs on the mind and on behavior; also known as medication and drug therapy.
Neurotransmitter	A neurotransmitter is a chemical that is used to relay, amplify and modulate electrical signals between a neurons and another cell.
Affect	A subjective feeling or emotional tone often accompanied by bodily expressions noticeable to others is called affect.
Nervous system	The body's electrochemical communication circuitry, made up of billions of neurons is a nervous system.
Norepinephrine	Norepinephrine is released from the adrenal glands as a hormone into the blood, but it is also a neurotransmitter in the nervous system. As a stress hormone, it affects parts of the human brain where attention and impulsivity are controlled. Along with epinephrine, this compound effects the fight-or-flight response, activating the sympathetic nervous system to directly increase heart rate, release energy from fat, and increase muscle readiness.
Dopamine	Dopamine is critical to the way the brain controls our movements and is a crucial part of the basal ganglia motor loop. It is commonly associated with the 'pleasure system' of the brain, providing feelings of enjoyment and reinforcement to motivate us to do, or continue doing, certain activities.
Receptor	A sensory receptor is a structure that recognizes a stimulus in the internal or external environment of an organism. In response to stimuli the sensory receptor initiates sensory transduction by creating graded potentials or action potentials in the same cell or in an adjacent one.
Antibody	An antibody is a protein used by the immune system to identify and neutralize foreign objects like bacteria and viruses. Each antibody recognizes a specific antigen unique to its target.
Antigen	An antigen is a molecule that stimulates the production of antibodies. Usually, it is a protein or a polysaccharide, but can be any type of molecule, including small molecules (haptens) coupled to a protein (carrier).
Protein	A protein is a complex, high-molecular-weight organic compound that consists of amino acids joined by peptide bonds. It is essential to the structure and function of all living cells and viruses. Many are enzymes or subunits of enzymes.
Enzyme	An enzyme is a protein that catalyzes, or speeds up, a chemical reaction. Enzymes are essential to sustain life because most chemical reactions in biological cells would occur too slowly, or would lead to different products, without enzymes.
Genetics	Genetics is the science of genes, heredity, and the variation of organisms.
Gene	A gene is an ultramicroscopic area of the chromosome. It is the smallest physical unit of the DNA molecule that carries a piece of hereditary information.
Nucleic acid	A nucleic acid is a complex, high-molecular-weight biochemical macromolecule composed of

	nucleotide chains that convey genetic information. The most common are deoxyribonucleic acid (DNA) and ribonucleic acid (RNA). Nucleic acids are found in all living cells and viruses.
Paradigm	Paradigm refers to the set of practices that defines a scientific discipline during a particular period of time. It provides a framework from which to conduct research, it ensures that a certain range of phenomena, those on which the paradigm focuses, are explored thoroughly. Itmay also blind scientists to other, perhaps more fruitful, ways of dealing with their subject matter.
Neurologist	A physician who studies the nervous system, especially its structure, functions, and abnormalities is referred to as neurologist.
Neuropsychol-gist	A psychologist concerned with the relationships among cognition, affect, behavior, and brain function is a neuropsychologist.
Psychological testing	Psychological testing is a field characterized by the use of small samples of behavior in order to infer larger generalizations about a given individual. The technical term for psychological testing is psychometrics.
Neuropsychol-gical test	A neuropsychological test use specifically designed tasks used to measure a psychological function known to be linked to a particular brain structure or pathway. They usually involve the systematic administration of clearly defined procedures in a formal environment.
Test battery	A group of tests and interviews given to the same individual is a test battery.
Standardized test	An oral or written assessment for which an individual receives a score indicating how the individual reponded relative to a previously tested large sample of others is referred to as a standardized test.
Control subjects	Control subjects are participants in an experiment who do not receive the treatment effect but for whom all other conditions are held comparable to those of experimental subjects.
Psychological deficit	The term used to indicate that performance of a pertinent psychological process is below that expected of a normal person is psychological deficit.
Intelligence quotient	An intelligence quotient is a score derived from a set of standardized tests that were developed with the purpose of measuring a person's cognitive abilities ("intelligence") in relation to their age group.
Wechsler	Wechsler is best known for his intelligence tests. The Wechsler Adult Intelligence Scale (WAIS) was developed first in 1939 and then called the Wechsler-Bellevue Intelligence Test. From these he derived the Wechsler Intelligence Scale for Children (WISC) in 1949 and the Wechsler Preschool and Primary Scale of Intelligence (WPPSI) in 1967. Wechsler originally created these tests to find out more about his patients at the Bellevue clinic and he found the then-current Binet IQ test unsatisfactory.
Wechsler Adult Intelligence Scale	Wechsler adult intelligence scale is an individual intelligence test for adults that yields separate verbal and performance IQ scores as well as an overall IQ score.
Wechsler adult Intelligence	Wechsler adult Intelligence Scale is a revision of the Wechsler-Bellevue test (1939), standardized for use with adults over the age of 16.
Lateralization	Lateralization refers to the dominance of one hemisphere of the brain for specific functions.
Left hemisphere	The left hemisphere of the cortex controls the right side of the body, coordinates complex movements, and, in 95% of people, controls the production of speech and written language.
Right hemisphere	The brain is divided into left and right cerebral hemispheres. The right hemisphere of the cortex controls the left side of the body.

Dichotic listening	Dichotic Listening is a procedure used for investigating selective attention in the auditory domain. Two messages are presented to both the left and right ears, normally using a set of headphones. Normally, participants are asked to pay attention to either one, or both of the messages and may later be asked about the content of both.
Explicit memory	Intentional or conscious recollection of information is referred to as explicit memory. Children under age three are usually poorest at explicit memory which may be due to the immaturity of the prefrontal lobes of the brain, which are believed to play an important role in memory for events.
Implicit memory	Implicit memory is the long-term memory of skills and procedures, or "how to" knowledge. It is often not easily verbalized, but can be used without consciously thinking about it.
Priming	A phenomenon in which exposure to a word or concept later makes it easier to recall related information, even when one has no conscious memory of the word or concept is called priming.
Frontal lobe	The frontal lobe comprises four major folds of cortical tissue: the precentral gyrus, superior gyrus and the middle gyrus of the frontal gyri, the inferior frontal gyrus. It has been found to play a part in impulse control, judgement, language, memory, motor function, problem solving, sexual behavior, socialization and spontaneity.
Lobes	The four major sections of the cerebral cortex: frontal, parietal, temporal, and occipital are called lobes.
Occipital lobe	The occipital lobe is the smallest of four true lobes in the human brain. Located in the rearmost portion of the skull, the occipital lobe is part of the forebrain structure. It is the visual processing center.
Perception	Perception is the process of acquiring, interpreting, selecting, and organizing sensory information.
Anxiety	Anxiety is a complex combination of the feeling of fear, apprehension and worry often accompanied by physical sensations such as palpitations, chest pain and/or shortness of breath.
Penis	The penis is the external male copulatory organ and the external male organ of urination. In humans, the penis is homologous to the female clitoris, as it develops from the same embryonic structure. It is capable of erection for use in copulation.
Ejaculation	Ejaculation is the process of ejecting semen from the penis, and is usually accompanied by orgasm as a result of sexual stimulation.
Conditioning	Conditioning describes the process by which behaviors can be learned or modified through interaction with the environment.
Learning	Learning is a relatively permanent change in behavior that results from experience. Thus, to attribute a behavioral change to learning, the change must be relatively permanent and must result from experience.
Learning paradigm	In abnormal psychology, the set of assumptions that abnormal behavior is learned in the same way as other human behavior is a learning paradigm.
Operant Conditioning	A simple form of learning in which an organism learns to engage in behavior because it is reinforced is referred to as operant conditioning. The consequences of a behavior produce changes in the probability of the behavior's occurence.
Pavlovian conditioning	Pavlovian conditioning, synonymous with classical conditioning is a type of learning found in animals, caused by the association (or pairing) of two stimuli or what Ivan Pavlov described as the learning of conditional behavior, therefore called conditioning.
Conditional	A conditional response is elicited by a conditional stimulus in a conditional reflex.

response	
Conditional stimulus	A conditional stimulus in a conditional reflex elicits a conditional response.
Neutral stimulus	A stimulus prior to conditioning that does not naturally result in the response of interest is called a neutral stimulus.
Reinforcement	In operant conditioning, reinforcement is any change in an environment that (a) occurs after the behavior, (b) seems to make that behavior re-occur more often in the future and (c) that reoccurence of behavior must be the result of the change.
Punishment	Punishment is the addtion of a stimulus that reduces the frequency of a response, or the removal of a stimulus that results in a reduction of the response.
Pleasure center	Olds and Milner discovered that electrical stimulation of a particular region in the Mesolimbic dopamine system was highly rewarding to rats; they believed they had discovered the pleasure center in the brain. It now appears that stimulation of many regions of the mesolimbic system can lead to rewarding effects--the key is that dopamine ultimately reaches neurons in the nucleus accumbens, a limbic system structure.
Conditioned taste aversion	A procedure in which an animal drinks a flavored solution and is then made sick by a toxin is conditioned taste aversion, called the Garcia Effect. Both the long time interval between CS and CR and that only a single trial is necessary for the conditioning challenges normal conditioning tenets.
Conditioned aversion	A learned dislike or conditioned negative emotional response to a particular stimulus is a conditioned aversion.
Chemotherapy	Chemotherapy is the use of chemical substances to treat disease. In its modern-day use, it refers almost exclusively to cytostatic drugs used to treat cancer.In its non-oncological use, the term may also refer to antibiotics.
Innate	Innate behavior is not learned or influenced by the environment, rather, it is present or predisposed at birth.
Pinel	Pinel is regarded as the father of modern psychiatry. He was a clinician believing that medical truth derived from clinical experience. While at Bicêtre, Pinel did away with bleeding, purging, and blistering in favor a therapy that involved close contact with and careful observation of patients.
Aversive stimulus	A stimulus that elicits pain, fear, or avoidance is an aversive stimulus.
Evolutionary perspective	A perspective that focuses on how humans have evolved and adapted behaviors required for survival against various environmental pressures over the long course is called the evolutionary perspective.
Physiological psychology	Physiological psychology refers to the study of the physiological mechanisms, in the brain and elsewhere, that mediate behavior and psychological experiences.

Illusion	An illusion is a distortion of a sensory perception.
Perception	Perception is the process of acquiring, interpreting, selecting, and organizing sensory information.
Receptor	A sensory receptor is a structure that recognizes a stimulus in the internal or external environment of an organism. In response to stimuli the sensory receptor initiates sensory transduction by creating graded potentials or action potentials in the same cell or in an adjacent one.
Neuron	The neuron is the primary cell of the nervous system. They are found in the brain, the spinal cord, in the nerves and ganglia of the peripheral nervous system. It is a specialized cell that conducts impulses through the nervous system and contains three major parts: cell body, dendrites, and an axon. It can have many dendrites but only one axon.
Visual cortex	The visual cortex is the general term applied to both the primary visual cortex and the visual association area. Anatomically, the visual cortex occupies the entire occipital lobe, the inferior temporal lobe (IT), posterior parts of the parietal lobe, and a few small regions in the frontal lobe.
Creativity	Creativity is the ability to think about something in novel and unusual ways and come up with unique solutions to problems. It involves divergent thinking, having many solutions or views to a problem.
Primary visual cortex	Primary visual cortex refers to the area at the rear of the occipital lobes where vision registers in the cerebral cortex.
Nocturnal	A person who exhibits nocturnal habits is referred to as a night owl.
Illumination	Illumination is the physical, objective measurement of light falling on a surface.
Adaptation	Adaptation is a lowering of sensitivity to a stimulus following prolonged exposure to that stimulus. Behavioral adaptations are special ways a particular organism behaves to survive in its natural habitat.
Theories	Theories are logically self-consistent models or frameworks describing the behavior of a certain natural or social phenomenon. They are broad explanations and predictions concerning phenomena of interest.
Brightness	The dimension of visual sensation that is dependent on the intensity of light reflected from a surface and that corresponds to the amplitude of the light wave is called brightness.
Retina	The retina is a thin layer of cells at the back of the eyeball. It is the part of the eye which converts light into nervous signals. The retina contains photoreceptor cells which receive the light; the resulting neural signals then undergo complex processing by other neurons of the retina, and are transformed into action potentials in retinal ganglion cells whose axons form the optic nerve.
Pupil	In the eye, the pupil is the opening in the middle of the iris. It appears black because most of the light entering it is absorbed by the tissues inside the eye. The size of the pupil is controlled by involuntary contraction and dilation of the iris, in order to regulate the intensity of light entering the eye. This is known as the pupillary reflex.
Iris	The iris is the most visible part of the eye. The iris is an annulus (or flattened ring) consisting of pigmented fibrovascular tissue known as a stroma. The stroma connects a sphincter muscle, which contracts the pupil, and a set of dialator muscles which open it.
Sclera	The sclera is the white outer coating of the eye made of tough fibrin connective tissue which gives the eye its shape and helps to protect the delicate inner parts.
Cornea	The cornea is the transparent front part of the eye that covers the iris, pupil, and anterior

	chamber and provides most of an eye's optical power. Together with the lens, the cornea refracts light and consequently helps the eye to focus.
Ciliary muscle	The ciliary muscle is a smooth muscle that affects zonules in the eye (fibers that suspend the lens in position during accommodation), enabling changes in lens shape for light focusing.
Accommodation	Piaget's developmental process of accommodation is the modification of currently held schemes or new schemes so that new information inconsistent with the existing schemes can be integrated and understood.
Construct	A generalized concept, such as anxiety or gravity, is a construct.
Binocular disparity	A binocular depth cue resulting from differences between the two retinal images formed of an object viewed at distances up to about 20 feet is referred to as binocular disparity.
Amacrine cells	Amacrine cells are interneurons in the retina which operate at the Inner Plexiform Layer (IPL), the second synaptic retinal layer where bipolar cells and ganglion cells synapse. Functionally, they are responsible for complex processing of the retinal image, specifically adjusting image brightness and, by integrating sequential activation of neurons, detecting motion.
Ganglion cell	A ganglion cell is a type of neuron located in the retina of the eye that receives visual information from photoreceptors via various intermediate cells such as bipolar cells, amacrine cells, and horizontal cells. Retinal ganglion cells' axons are myelinated.
Bipolar cell	As a part of the retina, the bipolar cell exists between photoreceptors and ganglion cells. Bipolar cells are so-named as they have a central body from which two sets of processes arise. At one end, they form synapses with either a single cone cell, or a number of rod cells. At the other end, they form synapses with ganglion cells, which fire action potentials along the optic nerve (cranial nerve II). They effectively transfer information from rods and cones to ganglion cells.
Ganglion	A ganglion is a tissue mass that contains the dendrites and cell bodies (or "somas") of nerve cells, in most case ones belonging to the peripheral nervous system. Within the central nervous system such a mass is often called a nucleus.
Horizontal cells	Horizontal cells are the laterally interconnecting neurons in the outer plexiform layer of the retina.
Blind spot	In anatomy, the blind spot is the region of the retina where the optic nerve and blood vessels pass through to connect to the back of the eye. Since there are no light receptors there, a part of the field of vision is not perceived.
Axon	An axon, or "nerve fiber," is a long slender projection of a nerve cell, or "neuron," which conducts electrical impulses away from the neuron's cell body or soma.
Fovea	The fovea, a part of the eye, is a spot located in the center of the macula. The fovea is responsible for sharp central vision, which is necessary in humans for reading, watching television or movies, driving, and any activity where visual detail is of primary importance.
Rod vision	Rod vision refers to the low-acuity, high-sensitivity, noncolor vision that occurs in dim light and is mediated by rods in the retina of the eye.
Species	Species refers to a reproductively isolated breeding population.
Cones	Cones are photoreceptors that transmit sensations of color, function in bright light, and used in visual acuity. Infants prior to months of age can only distinguish green and red indicating the cones are not fully developed; they can see all of the colors by 2 months of
Rods	Rods are cylindrical shaped photoreceptors that are sensitive to the intensity of light. Rods

	require less light to function than cone cells, and therefore are the primary source of visual information at night.
Duplexity	Duplexity refers to a theory stating that the retina has two kinds of photoreceptors.
Brain	The brain controls and coordinates most movement, behavior and homeostatic body functions such as heartbeat, blood pressure, fluid balance and body temperature. Functions of the brain are responsible for cognition, emotion, memory, motor learning and other sorts of learning. The brain is primarily made up of two types of cells: glia and neurons.
Stimulus	A change in an environmental condition that elicits a response is a stimulus.
Visible spectrum	The narrow band of electromagnetic waves, 380-760 nm in length, that are visible to the human eye is referred to as the visible spectrum.
Fixation	Fixation in abnormal psychology is the state where an individual becomes obsessed with an attachment to another human, animal or inanimate object. Fixation in vision refers to maintaining the gaze in a constant direction. .
Saccade	A saccade is a fast movement of an eye, head, or other part of an animal's body or of a device. It can also be a fast shift in frequency of an emitted signal, or other such fast change.
Transduction	Transduction in the nervous system typically refers to synaptic events wherein an electrical signal, known as an action potential, is converted into a chemical one via the release of neurotransmitters. Conversely, in sensory transduction a chemical or physical stimulus is transduced by sensory receptors into an electrical signal.
Rhodopsin	The photochemical in rods that undergoes structural changes in response to light and thereby initiates the transduction process for rod vision is rhodopsin. It most strongly absorbs green-blue light and therefore appears reddish-purple, which is why it is also called "visual purple".
Glutamate	Glutamate is one of the 20 standard amino acids used by all organisms in their proteins. It is critical for proper cell function, but it is not an essential nutrient in humans because it can be manufactured from other compounds.
Neurotransmitter	A neurotransmitter is a chemical that is used to relay, amplify and modulate electrical signals between a neurons and another cell.
Ion	An ion is an atom or group of atoms with a net electric charge. The energy required to detach an electron in its lowest energy state from an atom or molecule of a gas with less net electric charge is called the ionization potential, or ionization energy.
Striate cortex	The functionally defined primary visual cortex is approximately equivalent to the anatomically defined striate cortex located in the occipital lobe.
Thalamus	An area near the center of the brain involved in the relay of sensory information to the cortex and in the functions of sleep and attention is the thalamus.
Nucleus	In neuroanatomy, a cluster of cell bodies of neurons within the central nervous system is a nucleus.
Lateral geniculate nucleus	The lateral geniculate nucleus of the thalamus is a part of the brain, which is the primary processor of visual information, received from the retina, in the CNS.
Electrode	Any device used to electrically stimulate nerve tissue or to record its activity is an electrode.
Natural	Natural selection is a process by which biological populations are altered over time, as a

selection	result of the propagation of heritable traits that affect the capacity of individual organisms to survive and reproduce.
Homogeneous	In biology homogeneous has a meaning similar to its meaning in mathematics. Generally it means "the same" or "of the same quality or general property".
Mach band	A Mach band is an optical illusion. It is the region encircling a bright light which in visual perception appears lighter or darker than its surroundings, in a zone where the luminance increases or decreases rapidly.
Neural network	A clusters of neurons that is interconnected to process information is referred to as a neural network.
Receptive field	The receptive field of a sensory neuron is a region of sensitivity in which the presence of a stimulus will alter the firing of that neuron.
Brightness contrast	Brightness contrast refers to the perception of a difference in brightness as reflected from two different areas of the visual field.
Curare	Curare is a drug that once entered into the bloodstream and reaches the muscles it blocks the receptors on the muscles, paralyzing the muscles.
Cognition	The intellectual processes through which information is obtained, transformed, stored, retrieved, and otherwise used is cognition.
Simple cell	A neuron in the striate cortex that is maximally sensitive to the position and orientation of edges in the receptive field is called a simple cell.
Retinal disparity	A binocular cue for depth based on the difference in the image cast by an object on the retinas of the eyes as the object moves closer or farther away, is called retinal disparity.
Monocular	Depth perception combines several types of depth clues grouped into two categories: monocular clues, available from the input of just one eye, and binocular clues. Monocular clues include motion parallax, color vision, perspective, relative size, distance fog, depth from focus, and occlusion
Amino acid	Amino acid is the basic structural building unit of proteins. They form short polymer chains called peptides or polypeptides which in turn form structures called proteins.
Synapse	A synapse is specialized junction through which cells of the nervous system signal to one another and to non-neuronal cells such as muscles or glands.
Spatial frequency	The number of repetitions, per unit distance, of the repeating elements of the image of a pattern on the retina of the eye is called the spatial frequency.
Amplitude	Amplitude is a nonnegative scalar measure of a wave's magnitude of oscillation.
Hue	A hue refers to the gradation of color within the optical spectrum, or visible spectrum, of light. Hue may also refer to a particular color within this spectrum, as defined by its dominant wavelength, or the central tendency of its combined wavelengths.
Thomas Young	Thomas Young discovered that light was composed of waves through his famous double-slit experiment and described the process of accomodation of vision as a result of the change of the curvature of the lens. He also argued that color perception depends on the presence in the retina of three kinds of nerve fibres which respond respectively to red, green and violet light.
Helmholtz	Helmholtz a pioneer of the new science of psychology, was a rigorous experimental physiologist and philospher. He gave us the distinction betwen sensation and peception and is well known for his theories of color perception and hearing.
Trichromatic	The trichromatic theory was postulated by Young and later by Helmholtz. They demonstrated

theory	that most colors can be matched by superimposing three separate light sources known as primaries; a process known as additive mixing. The Young-Helmholtz theory of color vision was built around the assumption of there being three classes of receptors.
Encoding	Encoding refers to interpreting; transforming; modifying information so that it can be placed in memory. It is the first stage of information processing.
Hering	Hering disagreed with the trichromatic theory of color perception which held that the human eye perceived all colors in terms of three primary colors. (Red, Green, Blue). He believed that the visual system worked based on a system of color opponency, a system of six primary colors.
Hyperpolariz-tion	Hyperpolarization is any change in a cell's membrane potential that makes it more polarized. That is, hyperpolarization is an increase in the absolute value of a cell's membrane potential.
Behavioral observation	A form of behavioral assessment that entails careful observation of a person's overt behavior in a particular situation is behavioral observation.
Complementary colors	Pairs of colors that produce gray tones when added together are referred to as complementary colors. Due to the cytology of the human eye, all perceived colors are based on combinations of red, green, and blue.
Coding	In senation, coding is the process by which information about the quality and quantity of a stimulus is preserved in the pattern of action potentials sent through sensory neurons to the central nervous system.
Color constancy	Color constancy is an example of subjective constancy and a feature of the human color-perception system which ensures that the perceived color of objects remains relatively constant under varying illumination conditions in spite of physical change.
Enzyme	An enzyme is a protein that catalyzes, or speeds up, a chemical reaction. Enzymes are essential to sustain life because most chemical reactions in biological cells would occur too slowly, or would lead to different products, without enzymes.
Biopsychology	Biopsychology is the scientific study of the biological bases of behavior and mental states. Empirical experiments study changes in central nervous system activation in response to a stimulus.
Insight	Insight refers to a sudden awareness of the relationships among various elements that had previously appeared to be independent of one another.
Evolutionary perspective	A perspective that focuses on how humans have evolved and adapted behaviors required for survival against various environmental pressures over the long course is called the evolutionary perspective.
Visual perception	Visual perception is one of the senses, consisting of the ability to detect light and interpret it. Vision has a specific sensory system.
Neuroscience	A field that combines the work of psychologists, biologists, biochemists, medical researchers, and others in the study of the structure and function of the nervous system is neuroscience.

Perception | Perception is the process of acquiring, interpreting, selecting, and organizing sensory information.

Brain | The brain controls and coordinates most movement, behavior and homeostatic body functions such as heartbeat, blood pressure, fluid balance and body temperature. Functions of the brain are responsible for cognition, emotion, memory, motor learning and other sorts of learning. The brain is primarily made up of two types of cells: glia and neurons.

Association cortex | Region of the cerebral cortex in which the highest intellectual functions, including thinking and problem solving, occur is the association cortex.

Parallel processing | The simultaneous distribution of information across different neural pathways is called parallel processing.

Receptor | A sensory receptor is a structure that recognizes a stimulus in the internal or external environment of an organism. In response to stimuli the sensory receptor initiates sensory transduction by creating graded potentials or action potentials in the same cell or in an adjacent one.

Neuron | The neuron is the primary cell of the nervous system. They are found in the brain, the spinal cord, in the nerves and ganglia of the peripheral nervous system. It is a specialized cell that conducts impulses through the nervous system and contains three major parts: cell body, dendrites, and an axon. It can have many dendrites but only one axon.

Visual acuity | Visual acuity is the eye's ability to detect fine details and is the quantitative measure of the eye's ability to see an in-focus image at a certain distance.

Sensation | Sensation is the first stage in the chain of biochemical and neurologic events that begins with the impinging of a stimulus upon the receptor cells of a sensory organ, which then leads to perception, the mental state that is reflected in statements like "I see a uniformly blue wall."

Visual perception | Visual perception is one of the senses, consisting of the ability to detect light and interpret it. Vision has a specific sensory system.

Homogeneous | In biology homogeneous has a meaning similar to its meaning in mathematics. Generally it means "the same" or "of the same quality or general property".

Association areas | Association areas refer to the site of the higher mental processes such as thought, language, memory, and speech.

Cerebral cortex | The cerebral cortex is the outermost layer of the cerebrum and has a grey color. It is made up of four lobes and it is involved in many complex brain functions including memory, perceptual awareness, "thinking", language and consciousness. The cerebral cortex receives sensory information from many different sensory organs eg: eyes, ears, etc. and processes the information.

Feedback | Feedback refers to information returned to a person about the effects a response has had.

Sensory neuron | A sensory neuron is an afferent nerve cell within the nervous system responsible for converting external stimuli from the organism's environment into internal electrical impulses. It carries messages from a sensory organ, through a nerve, into the brain or spinal cord.

Attention | Attention is the cognitive process of selectively concentrating on one thing while ignoring other things. Psychologists have labeled three types of attention: sustained attention, selective attention, and divided attention.

Occipital lobe | The occipital lobe is the smallest of four true lobes in the human brain. Located in the rearmost portion of the skull, the occipital lobe is part of the forebrain structure. It is

	the visual processing center.
Visual cortex	The visual cortex is the general term applied to both the primary visual cortex and the visual association area. Anatomically, the visual cortex occupies the entire occipital lobe, the inferior temporal lobe (IT), posterior parts of the parietal lobe, and a few small regions in the frontal lobe.
Lobes	The four major sections of the cerebral cortex: frontal, parietal, temporal, and occipital are called lobes.
Primary visual cortex	Primary visual cortex refers to the area at the rear of the occipital lobes where vision registers in the cerebral cortex.
Longitudinal fissure	The longitudinal fissure is the fissure (groove) that runs from the rostral to caudal portion of the brain, that serves to separate the left and right hemispheres
Temporal lobe	The temporal lobe is part of the cerebrum. It lies at the side of the brain, beneath the lateral or Sylvian fissure. Adjacent areas in the superior, posterior and lateral parts of the temporal lobe are involved in high-level auditory processing.
Receptive field	The receptive field of a sensory neuron is a region of sensitivity in which the presence of a stimulus will alter the firing of that neuron.
Scotoma	The Scotoma is an area of loss of visual acuity surrounded by a field of normal or relatively well-preserved vision. Every normal eye has a scotoma in its field of vision, usually termed its blind spot. Others may occur from damage.
Fixation	Fixation in abnormal psychology is the state where an individual becomes obsessed with an attachment to another human, animal or inanimate object. Fixation in vision refers to maintaining the gaze in a constant direction. .
Blindsight	Blindsight is residual visual sensitivity independent of any subjective experience of visual perception. A person experiencing blindsight, if not consciously able to see, is still influenced by objects in his field of vision.
Lashley	Lashley failed to find a single biological locus of memory suggesting to him that memories were not localized to one part of the brain, but were widely distributed throughout the cortex.
Striate cortex	The functionally defined primary visual cortex is approximately equivalent to the anatomically defined striate cortex located in the occipital lobe.
Theories	Theories are logically self-consistent models or frameworks describing the behavior of a certain natural or social phenomenon. They are broad explanations and predictions concerning phenomena of interest.
Lesion	A lesion is a non-specific term referring to abnormal tissue in the body. It can be caused by any disease process including trauma (physical, chemical, electrical), infection, neoplasm, metabolic and autoimmune.
Positron emission tomography	Positron Emission Tomography measures emissions from radioactively labeled chemicals that have been injected into the bloodstream. The greatest benefit is that different compounds can show blood flow and oxygen and glucose metabolism in the tissues of the working brain.
Ventral stream	The primate visual system consists of about thirty areas of the cerebral cortex called the visual cortex. The visual cortex is divided into the ventral stream and the dorsal stream. The ventral stream is associated with object recognition and form representation.
Dorsal stream	The dorsal stream is a pathway for visual information which flows through the visual cortex, the part of the brain which provides visual processing. It is involved in spatial awareness: recognizing where objects are in space.

Right hemisphere	The brain is divided into left and right cerebral hemispheres. The right hemisphere of the cortex controls the left side of the body.
Variability	Statistically, variability refers to how much the scores in a distribution spread out, away from the mean.
Dissociation	Dissociation is a psychological state or condition in which certain thoughts, emotions, sensations, or memories are separated from the rest.
Correlation	A statistical technique for determining the degree of association between two or more variables is referred to as correlation.
Schema	Schema refers to a way of mentally representing the world, such as a belief or an expectation, that can influence perception of persons, objects, and situations.
Prosopagnosia	Prosopagnosia is a rare disorder of face perception where the ability to recognize faces is impaired, although the ability to recognize objects may be relatively intact.
Visual agnosia	Visual Agnosia is the inability of the brain to make sense of or make use of some part of otherwise normal visual stimulus, and is typified by the inability to recognize familiar objects or faces.
Agnosia	Agnosia is a loss of ability to recognize objects, persons, sounds, shapes or smells while the specific sense is not defective nor is there any significant memory loss.
Species	Species refers to a reproductively isolated breeding population.
Hypothesis	A specific statement about behavior or mental processes that is testable through research is a hypothesis.
Organ of Corti	The Organ of Corti is the hearing organ of the inner ear. It contains receptors that respond to vibrations in the basilar membrane which are caused by sound.
Basilar membrane	The basilar membrane within the cochlea of the inner ear is the part of the auditory system that decomposes incoming auditory signals into their frequency components. This allows higher neural processing of sound information to focus on the frequency spectrum of input, rather than just the time domain waveform.
Hair cells	Hair cells are the sensory cells of both the auditory system and the vestibular system. The auditory hair cells are located within the organ of Corti on a thin basilar membrane in the cochlea of the inner ear.
Coding	In senation, coding is the process by which information about the quality and quantity of a stimulus is preserved in the pattern of action potentials sent through sensory neurons to the central nervous system.
Cochlea	The Cochlea is the bony tube that contains the basilar membrane and the organ of Corti. The cochlea consists of three fluid-filled chambers - scala tympani and scala vestibuli and scala media.
Auditory system	The auditory system is the sensory system for the sense of hearing. On its path from the outside world to the forebrain, sound information is preserved and modified in many ways. It changes media twice, first from air to fluid, then from fluid to action potentials.
Vestibular system	The vestibular system, or balance system, is the sensory system that provides the dominant input about our movement and orientation in space. Together with the cochlea, the auditory organ, it is situated in the vestibulum in the inner ear.
Primary auditory cortex	The primary auditory cortex is responsible for processing of auditory information. It is located in the temporal lobe; the posterior half of the superior temporal gyrus and also dives into the lateral sulcus as the transverse temporal gyri.

Lateral fissure — The lateral fissure is one of the most prominent structures of the human brain. It divides the frontal lobe and parietal lobe above from the temporal lobe below.

Auditory nerve — The vestibulocochlear nerve is the eighth of twelve cranial nerves, and also known as the auditory nerve. It is the nerve along which the sensory cells (the hair cells) of the inner ear transmit information to the brain. It consists of the cochlear nerve, carrying information about hearing, and the vestibular nerve, carrying information about balance.

Thalamus — An area near the center of the brain involved in the relay of sensory information to the cortex and in the functions of sleep and attention is the thalamus.

Synapse — A synapse is specialized junction through which cells of the nervous system signal to one another and to non-neuronal cells such as muscles or glands.

Nucleus — In neuroanatomy, a cluster of cell bodies of neurons within the central nervous system is a nucleus.

Nerve — A nerve is an enclosed, cable-like bundle of nerve fibers or axons, which includes the glia that ensheath the axons in myelin. Neurons are sometimes called nerve cells, though this term is technically imprecise since many neurons do not form nerves.

Axon — An axon, or "nerve fiber," is a long slender projection of a nerve cell, or "neuron," which conducts electrical impulses away from the neuron's cell body or soma.

Sound localization — Sound localization is a listener's ability to identify the location of origin of a detected sound. There are two general methods for sound localization, binaural cues and monaural cues.

Amplitude — Amplitude is a nonnegative scalar measure of a wave's magnitude of oscillation.

Nocturnal — A person who exhibits nocturnal habits is referred to as a night owl.

Somatosensory — Somatosensory system consists of the various sensory receptors that trigger the experiences labelled as touch or pressure, temperature, pain, and the sensations of muscle movement and joint position including posture, movement, and facial expression.

Senses — The senses are systems that consist of a sensory cell type that respond to a specific kind of physical energy, and that correspond to a defined region within the brain where the signals are received and interpreted.

Somatosensory system — Somatosensory system consists of the various sensory receptors that trigger the experiences labelled as touch or pressure, temperature, pain, and the sensations of muscle movement and joint position including posture, movement, and facial expression.

Free nerve ending — A free nerve ending is an unspecialized, afferent nerve ending. It is unencapsulated and no complex sensory structures exists, such as those found in Meissner's corpuscle or Pacinian corpuscle. They are the most common type of nerve ending, and are most frequently found in the skin. They are responsible for detecting temperature, mechanical stimuli (such as pressure), touch and pain (nociception).

Displacement — An unconscious defense mechanism in which the individual directs aggressive or sexual feelings away from the primary object to someone or something safe is referred to as displacement. Displacement in linguistics is simply the ability to talk about things not present.

Spinal cord — The spinal cord is a part of the vertebrate nervous system that is enclosed in and protected by the vertebral column (it passes through the spinal canal). It consists of nerve cells. The spinal cord carries sensory signals and motor innervation to most of the skeletal muscles in the body.

Proprioception — Proprioception is the sense of the position of parts of the body, relative to other neighboring parts of the body.

Somatosensory cortex | The primary somatosensory cortex is across the central sulcus and behind the primary motor cortex configured to generally correspond with the arrangement of nearby motor cells related to specific body parts. It is the main sensory receptive area for the sense of touch.

Neuroscience | A field that combines the work of psychologists, biologists, biochemists, medical researchers, and others in the study of the structure and function of the nervous system is neuroscience.

Reticular formation | Reticular formation is a part of the brain which is involved in stereotypical actions, such as walking, sleeping, and lying down. The reticular formation, phylogenetically one of the oldest portions of the brain, is a poorly-differentiated area of the brain stem.

Chronic | Chronic refers to a relatively long duration, usually more than a few months.

Stages | Stages represent relatively discrete periods of time in which functioning is qualitatively different from functioning at other periods.

Gyrus | A gyrus is a ridge on the cerebral cortex. It is generally surrounded by one or more sulci.

Somatosensation | Somatosensation consists of the various sensory receptors that trigger the experiences labelled as touch or pressure, temperature (warm or cold), pain (including itch and tickle), and the sensations of muscle movement and joint position including posture, movement, and facial expression (collectively also called proprioception).

Tactile | Pertaining to the sense of touch is referred to as tactile.

Discrimination | In Learning theory, discrimination refers the ability to distinguish between a conditioned stimulus and other stimuli. It can be brought about by extensive training or differential reinforcement. In social terms, it is the denial of privileges to a person or a group on the basis of prejudice.

Parietal lobe | The parietal lobe is positioned above (superior to) the occipital lobe and behind (posterior to) the frontal lobe. It plays important roles in integrating sensory information from various senses, and in the manipulation of objects.

Paradoxical | Paradoxical intention refers to instructing clients to do the opposite of the desired behavior. Telling an impotent man not to have sex or an insomniac not to sleep reduces anxiety to perform.

Stimulus | A change in an environmental condition that elicits a response is a stimulus.

Congenital | A condition existing at birth is referred to as congenital.

Trauma | Trauma refers to a severe physical injury or wound to the body caused by an external force, or a psychological shock having a lasting effect on mental life.

Cingulate gyrus | Cingulate gyrus is a gyrus in the medial part of the brain. It partially wraps around the corpus callosum and is limited above by the cingulate sulcus. It functions as an intergral part of the limbic system, which is involved with emotion formation and processing, learning, and memory.

Illusion | An illusion is a distortion of a sensory perception.

Cingulate cortex | The part of the limbic system that is believed to process cognitive information in emotion is the cingulate cortex. The cingulate cortex is part of the brain and situated roughly in the middle of the cortex.

Threshold | In general, a threshold is a fixed location or value where an abrupt change is observed. In the sensory modalities, it is the minimum amount of stimulus energy necessary to elicit a sensory response.

Lobotomy | A lobotomy is the intentional severing of the prefrontal cortex from the thalamic region of

the brain. The frontal lobe of the brain controls a number of advanced cognitive functions, as well as motor control. Today, lobotomy is very infrequently practised. It may be a treatment of last resort for obsessive-compulsive sufferers, and may also be used for people suffering chronic pain.

Interneurons — Interneurons are the neurons that provide connections between sensory and motor neurons, as well as between themselves.

Interneuron — An interneuron (also called relay neuron or association neuron) is a neuron that communicates only to other neurons.

Analgesia — Analgesia refers to insensitivity to pain without loss of consciousness.

Chemical senses — Chemical senses include smell and taste.

Gustation — Gustation is the direct detection of chemical composition, usually through contact with chemoreceptor cells in a liquid medium. It is very similar to olfaction, in which the chemical composition of an organism's ambient medium is detected by chemoreceptors.

Olfaction — Olfaction, the sense of odor (smell), is the detection of chemicals dissolved in air. Smells are sensed by the olfactory epithelium located in the nose and processed by the olfactory system.

Olfactory system — The olfactory system is the sensory system used for the sense of smell. The olfactory system is often spoken of along with the gustatory system as the chemosensory senses because both transduce chemical signals into perception

Gustatory system — The gustatory system is the sensory system that uses taste buds on the upper surface of the tongue to provide information about the taste of food being eaten.

Physiology — The study of the functions and activities of living cells, tissues, and organs and of the physical and chemical phenomena involved is referred to as physiology.

Pheromone — A pheromone is any chemical produced by a living organism that transmits a message to other members of the same species. There are alarm pheromones, food trail pheromones, sex pheromones, and many others. Their use among insects has been particularly well documented, although many vertebrates also communicate using pheromones. Their use by humans is controversial.

Learning — Learning is a relatively permanent change in behavior that results from experience. Thus, to attribute a behavioral change to learning, the change must be relatively permanent and must result from experience.

Protein — A protein is a complex, high-molecular-weight organic compound that consists of amino acids joined by peptide bonds. It is essential to the structure and function of all living cells and viruses. Many are enzymes or subunits of enzymes.

Olfactory mucosa — The olfactory mucosa is an organ made up of the olfactory epithelium and the mucosa, or mucus secreting glands, behind the epithelium. The mucus protects the olfactory epithelium and allows odors to dissolve so that they can be detected by olfactory receptor neurons.

Amygdala — Located in the brain's medial temporal lobe, the almond-shaped amygdala is believed to play a key role in the emotions. It forms part of the limbic system and is linked to both fear responses and pleasure. Its size is positively correlated with aggressive behavior across species.

Olfactory bulb — The olfactory bulb is a part of the brain that is a distinct outgrowth from the forebrain. It plays a major role in olfaction, which is the perception of smells. The olfactory bulb receives direct input from olfactory nerve, made up of the axons from approximately 10 million olfactory receptor neurons in the olfactory mucosa, a region of the nasal cavity.

Limbic system | The limbic system is a group of brain structures that are involved in various emotions such as aggression, fear, pleasure and also in the formation of memory. The limbic system affects the endocrine system and the autonomic nervous system. It consists of several subcortical structures located around the thalamus.

Projection | Attributing one's own undesirable thoughts, impulses, traits, or behaviors to others is referred to as projection.

Frontal lobe | The frontal lobe comprises four major folds of cortical tissue: the precentral gyrus, superior gyrus and the middle gyrus of the frontal gyri, the inferior frontal gyrus. It has been found to play a part in impulse control, judgement, language, memory, motor function, problem solving, sexual behavior, socialization and spontaneity.

Taste bud | The taste bud (or lingual papillae) is a small structure on the upper surface of the tongue that provides information about the taste of food being eaten. It is known that there are five taste sensations: Sweet, Bitter, Umami, Salty and Sour.

Papillae | The bumps on the tongue that contain taste buds, the receptors for taste, are papillae.

Cranial nerves | Cranial nerves are nerves that emerge from the brainstem instead of the spinal cord. Cranial nerves I and II are named as such, but are technically not nerves, as they are continuations of the central nervous system.

Cranial nerve | A Cranial nerve emerges from the brainstem instead of the spinal cord.

Ion channel | An Ion channel is a pore-forming protein that help establish the small voltage gradient that exists across the membrane of all living cells, by controlling the flow of ions. They are present in the membranes that surround all biological cells.

Ion | An ion is an atom or group of atoms with a net electric charge. The energy required to detach an electron in its lowest energy state from an atom or molecule of a gas with less net electric charge is called the ionization potential, or ionization energy.

Afferent neurons | Afferent neurons transmit messages from sensory receptors to the spinal cord and brain.

Homunculus | Homunculus is a term used in a number of ways to describe systems that are thought of as being run by a "little man" inside. For instance, the homunculus continues to be considered as one of the major theories on the origin of consciousness, that there is a part in the brain whose purpose is to be "you".

Anosmia | Anosmia is the lack of olfaction, or a loss of the sense of smell. It can be either temporary or permanent.

Olfactory nerve | The olfactory nerve is the first of twelve cranial nerves. It consists of a collection of sensory nerve fibers that extend down from the olfactory bulb and pass through the many openings of the cribriform plate, a sieve-like structure. The specialized olfactory receptor neurons of the olfactory nerve are located in the olfactory mucosa of the upper parts of the nasal cavity.

Down syndrome | Down syndrome encompasses a number of genetic disorders, of which trisomy 21 (a nondisjunction, the so-called extrachromosone) is the most representative, causing highly variable degrees of learning difficulties as well as physical disabilities. Incidence of Down syndrome is estimated at 1 per 660 births, making it the most common chromosomal abnormality.

Epilepsy | Epilepsy is a chronic neurological condition characterized by recurrent unprovoked neural discharges. It is commonly controlled with medication, although surgical methods are used as well.

Syndrome | The term syndrome is the association of several clinically recognizable features, signs, symptoms, phenomena or characteristics which often occur together, so that the presence of

	one feature indicates the presence of the others.
Multiple sclerosis	Multiple sclerosis affects neurons, the cells of the brain and spinal cord that carry information, create thought and perception, and allow the brain to control the body. Surrounding and protecting these neurons is a layer of fat, called myelin, which helps neurons carry electrical signals. MS causes gradual destruction of myelin (demyelination) in patches throughout the brain and/or spinal cord, causing various symptoms depending upon which signals are interrupted.
Blocking	If the one of the two members of a compound stimulus fails to produce the CR due to an earlier conditioning of the other member of the compound stimulus, blocking has occurred.
Selective attention	Selective attention is a type of attention which involves focusing on a specific aspect of a scene while ignoring other aspects.
Consciousness	The awareness of the sensations, thoughts, and feelings being experienced at a given moment is called consciousness.
Biopsychologist	A psychologist who studies the relationship between behavior and biological processes, especially activity in the nervous system is referred to as a Biopsychologist.

Somatosensory	Somatosensory system consists of the various sensory receptors that trigger the experiences labelled as touch or pressure, temperature, pain, and the sensations of muscle movement and joint position including posture, movement, and facial expression.
Sensorimotor	The first of Piaget's stages is the Sensorimotor stage. This stage typically ranges from birth to 2 years. In this stage, children experience the world through their senses. During this stage, object permanence and stranger anxiety develop.
Automaticity	The ability to process information with little or no effort is referred to as automaticity.
Learning	Learning is a relatively permanent change in behavior that results from experience. Thus, to attribute a behavioral change to learning, the change must be relatively permanent and must result from experience.
Association cortex	Region of the cerebral cortex in which the highest intellectual functions, including thinking and problem solving, occur is the association cortex.
Receptor	A sensory receptor is a structure that recognizes a stimulus in the internal or external environment of an organism. In response to stimuli the sensory receptor initiates sensory transduction by creating graded potentials or action potentials in the same cell or in an adjacent one.
Feedback	Feedback refers to information returned to a person about the effects a response has had.
Nerve	A nerve is an enclosed, cable-like bundle of nerve fibers or axons, which includes the glia that ensheath the axons in myelin. Neurons are sometimes called nerve cells, though this term is technically imprecise since many neurons do not form nerves.
Stages	Stages represent relatively discrete periods of time in which functioning is qualitatively different from functioning at other periods.
Pinel	Pinel is regarded as the father of modern psychiatry. He was a clinician believing that medical truth derived from clinical experience. While at Bicêtre, Pinel did away with bleeding, purging, and blistering in favor a therapy that involved close contact with and careful observation of patients.
Nervous system	The body's electrochemical communication circuitry, made up of billions of neurons is a nervous system.
Motor cortex	Motor cortex refers to the section of cortex that lies in the frontal lobe, just across the central fissure from the sensory cortex. Neural impulses in the motor cortex are linked to muscular responses throughout the body.
Prefrontal cortex	The prefrontal cortex is the anterior part of the frontal lobes of the brain, lying in front of the motor and associative areas. It has been implicated in planning complex cognitive behaviors, personality expression and moderating correct social behavior. The prefrontal cortex continues to develop until around age 6.
Attention	Attention is the cognitive process of selectively concentrating on one thing while ignoring other things. Psychologists have labeled three types of attention: sustained attention, selective attention, and divided attention.
Perception	Perception is the process of acquiring, interpreting, selecting, and organizing sensory information.
Somatosensory system	Somatosensory system consists of the various sensory receptors that trigger the experiences labelled as touch or pressure, temperature, pain, and the sensations of muscle movement and joint position including posture, movement, and facial expression.
Auditory system	The auditory system is the sensory system for the sense of hearing. On its path from the outside world to the forebrain, sound information is preserved and modified in many ways. It

	changes media twice, first from air to fluid, then from fluid to action potentials.
Left hemisphere	The left hemisphere of the cortex controls the right side of the body, coordinates complex movements, and, in 95% of people, controls the production of speech and written language.
Right hemisphere	The brain is divided into left and right cerebral hemispheres. The right hemisphere of the cortex controls the left side of the body.
Apraxia	Apraxia is a neurological disorder characterized by loss of the ability to execute or carry out learned movements, despite having the desire and the physical ability to perform the movements.
Motivation	In psychology, motivation is the driving force (desire) behind all actions of an organism.
Watson	Watson, the father of behaviorism, developed the term "Behaviorism" as a name for his proposal to revolutionize the study of human psychology in order to put it on a firm experimental footing.
Parietal lobe	The parietal lobe is positioned above (superior to) the occipital lobe and behind (posterior to) the frontal lobe. It plays important roles in integrating sensory information from various senses, and in the manipulation of objects.
Lesion	A lesion is a non-specific term referring to abnormal tissue in the body. It can be caused by any disease process including trauma (physical, chemical, electrical), infection, neoplasm, metabolic and autoimmune.
Stroke	A stroke occurs when the blood supply to a part of the brain is suddenly interrupted by occlusion, by hemorrhage, or other causes
Brain	The brain controls and coordinates most movement, behavior and homeostatic body functions such as heartbeat, blood pressure, fluid balance and body temperature. Functions of the brain are responsible for cognition, emotion, memory, motor learning and other sorts of learning. The brain is primarily made up of two types of cells: glia and neurons.
Projection	Attributing one's own undesirable thoughts, impulses, traits, or behaviors to others is referred to as projection.
Neuron	The neuron is the primary cell of the nervous system. They are found in the brain, the spinal cord, in the nerves and ganglia of the peripheral nervous system. It is a specialized cell that conducts impulses through the nervous system and contains three major parts: cell body, dendrites, and an axon. It can have many dendrites but only one axon.
Frontal lobe	The frontal lobe comprises four major folds of cortical tissue: the precentral gyrus, superior gyrus and the middle gyrus of the frontal gyri, the inferior frontal gyrus. It has been found to play a part in impulse control, judgement, language, memory, motor function, problem solving, sexual behavior, socialization and spontaneity.
Lateral fissure	The lateral fissure is one of the most prominent structures of the human brain. It divides the frontal lobe and parietal lobe above from the temporal lobe below.
Longitudinal fissure	The longitudinal fissure is the fissure (groove) that runs from the rostral to caudal portion of the brain, that serves to separate the left and right hemispheres
Cingulate gyrus	Cingulate gyrus is a gyrus in the medial part of the brain. It partially wraps around the corpus callosum and is limited above by the cingulate sulcus. It functions as an intergral part of the limbic system, which is involved with emotion formation and processing, learning, and memory.
Gyrus	A gyrus is a ridge on the cerebral cortex. It is generally surrounded by one or more sulci.
Theories	Theories are logically self-consistent models or frameworks describing the behavior of a

	certain natural or social phenomenon. They are broad explanations and predictions concerning phenomena of interest.
Receptive field	The receptive field of a sensory neuron is a region of sensitivity in which the presence of a stimulus will alter the firing of that neuron.
Penfield	Penfield treated patients with severe epilepsy by destroying nerve cells in the brain. Before operating, he stimulated the brain with electrical probes while the patients were conscious on the operating table, and observed their responses. It allowed him to create maps of sensory and motor functions.
Homunculus	Homunculus is a term used in a number of ways to describe systems that are thought of as being run by a "little man" inside. For instance, the homunculus continues to be considered as one of the major theories on the origin of consciousness, that there is a part in the brain whose purpose is to be "you".
Somatosensory cortex	The primary somatosensory cortex is across the central sulcus and behind the primary motor cortex configured to generally correspond with the arrangement of nearby motor cells related to specific body parts. It is the main sensory receptive area for the sense of touch.
Adaptation	Adaptation is a lowering of sensitivity to a stimulus following prolonged exposure to that stimulus. Behavioral adaptations are special ways a particular organism behaves to survive in its natural habitat.
Cerebral cortex	The cerebral cortex is the outermost layer of the cerebrum and has a grey color. It is made up of four lobes and it is involved in many complex brain functions including memory, perceptual awareness, "thinking", language and consciousness. The cerebral cortex receives sensory information from many different sensory organs eg: eyes, ears, etc. and processes the information.
Cerebellum	The cerebellum is located in the inferior posterior portion of the head (the hindbrain), directly dorsal to the brainstem and pons, inferior to the occipital lobe. The cerebellum is a region of the brain that plays an important role in the integration of sensory perception and fine motor output.
Basal ganglia	The basal ganglia are a group of nuclei in the brain associated with motor and learning functions.
Visual cortex	The visual cortex is the general term applied to both the primary visual cortex and the visual association area. Anatomically, the visual cortex occupies the entire occipital lobe, the inferior temporal lobe (IT), posterior parts of the parietal lobe, and a few small regions in the frontal lobe.
Brain stem	The brain stem is the stalk of the brain below the cerebral hemispheres. It is the major route for communication between the forebrain and the spinal cord and peripheral nerves. It also controls various functions including respiration, regulation of heart rhythms, and primary aspects of sound localization.
Vestibular system	The vestibular system, or balance system, is the sensory system that provides the dominant input about our movement and orientation in space. Together with the cochlea, the auditory organ, it is situated in the vestibulum in the inner ear.
Amplitude	Amplitude is a nonnegative scalar measure of a wave's magnitude of oscillation.
Tremor	Tremor is the rhythmic, oscillating shaking movement of the whole body or just a certain part of it, caused by problems of the neurons responsible from muscle action.
Brain imaging	Brain imaging is a fairly recent discipline within medicine and neuroscience. Brain imaging falls into two broad categories -- structural imaging and functional imaging.

Heterogeneous	A heterogeneous compound, mixture, or other such object is one that consists of many different items, which are often not easily sorted or separated, though they are clearly distinct.
Lobes	The four major sections of the cerebral cortex: frontal, parietal, temporal, and occipital are called lobes.
Anatomy	Anatomy is the branch of biology that deals with the structure and organization of living things. It can be divided into animal anatomy (zootomy) and plant anatomy (phytonomy). Major branches of anatomy include comparative anatomy, histology, and human anatomy.
Thalamus	An area near the center of the brain involved in the relay of sensory information to the cortex and in the functions of sleep and attention is the thalamus.
Motor neuron	A motor neuron is an efferent neuron that originates in the spinal cord and synapses with muscle fibers to facilitate muscle contraction and with muscle spindles to modify proprioceptive sensitivity.
Spinal cord	The spinal cord is a part of the vertebrate nervous system that is enclosed in and protected by the vertebral column (it passes through the spinal canal). It consists of nerve cells. The spinal cord carries sensory signals and motor innervation to most of the skeletal muscles in the body.
Modulation	Modulation is the process of varying a carrier signal, typically a sinusoidal signal, in order to use that signal to convey information.
Interneurons	Interneurons are the neurons that provide connections between sensory and motor neurons, as well as between themselves.
Gray matter	Gray matter is a category of nervous tissue with many nerve cell bodies and few myelinated axons. Generally, gray matter can be understood as the parts of the brain responsible for information processing; whereas, white matter is responsible for information transmission. In addition, gray matter does not have a myelin sheath and does not regenerate after injury unlike white matter.
Interneuron	An interneuron (also called relay neuron or association neuron) is a neuron that communicates only to other neurons.
Synapse	A synapse is specialized junction through which cells of the nervous system signal to one another and to non-neuronal cells such as muscles or glands.
Distal	Students can set both long-term (distal) and short-term (proximal) goals .
Axon	An axon, or "nerve fiber," is a long slender projection of a nerve cell, or "neuron," which conducts electrical impulses away from the neuron's cell body or soma.
Midbrain	Located between the hindbrain and forebrain, a region in which many nerve-fiber systems ascend and descend to connect the higher and lower portions of the brain is referred to as midbrain. It is archipallian in origin, meaning its general architecture is shared with the most ancient of vertebrates. Dopamine produced in the subtantia nigra plays a role in motivation and habituation of species from humans to the most elementary animals such as insects.
Nucleus	In neuroanatomy, a cluster of cell bodies of neurons within the central nervous system is a nucleus.
Cranial nerves	Cranial nerves are nerves that emerge from the brainstem instead of the spinal cord. Cranial nerves I and II are named as such, but are technically not nerves, as they are continuations of the central nervous system.
Cranial nerve	A Cranial nerve emerges from the brainstem instead of the spinal cord.

White matter	White matter is one of the two main solid components of the central nervous system. It is composed of axons which connect various grey matter areas of the brain to each other and carry nerve impulses between neurons.
Proximal	Students can set both long-term (distal) and short-term (proximal) goals .
Inner ear	The inner ear consists of the oval window, cochlea, and basilar membrane.
Species	Species refers to a reproductively isolated breeding population.
Reticular formation	Reticular formation is a part of the brain which is involved in stereotypical actions, such as walking, sleeping, and lying down. The reticular formation, phylogenetically one of the oldest portions of the brain, is a poorly-differentiated area of the brain stem.
Semicircular canals	The semicircular canals are three half-circular, interconnected tubes located inside each ear that are the equivalent of three gyroscopes located in three planes perpendicular (at right angles) to each other.
Skeletal muscle	Skeletal muscle is a type of striated muscle, attached to the skeleton. They are used to facilitate movement, by applying force to bones and joints; via contraction. They generally contract voluntarily (via nerve stimulation), although they can contract involuntarily.
Golgi	Golgi discovered a method of staining nervous tissue which would stain a limited number of cells at random, in their entirety. This enabled him to view the paths of nerve cells in the brain for the first time. He called his discovery the black reaction. It is now known universally as the Golgi stain.
Central nervous system	The vertebrate central nervous system consists of the brain and spinal cord.
Reflex	A simple, involuntary response to a stimulus is referred to as reflex. Reflex actions originate at the spinal cord rather than the brain.
Afferent neurons	Afferent neurons transmit messages from sensory receptors to the spinal cord and brain.
Stimulus	A change in an environmental condition that elicits a response is a stimulus.
Agonist	Agonist refers to a drug that mimics or increases a neurotransmitter's effects.
Sensory neuron	A sensory neuron is an afferent nerve cell within the nervous system responsible for converting external stimuli from the organism's environment into internal electrical impulses. It carries messages from a sensory organ, through a nerve, into the brain or spinal cord.
Ventral stream	The primate visual system consists of about thirty areas of the cerebral cortex called the visual cortex. The visual cortex is divided into the ventral stream and the dorsal stream. The ventral stream is associated with object recognition and form representation.
Dorsal stream	The dorsal stream is a pathway for visual information which flows through the visual cortex, the part of the brain which provides visual processing. It is involved in spatial awareness: recognizing where objects are in space.
Visual perception	Visual perception is one of the senses, consisting of the ability to detect light and interpret it. Vision has a specific sensory system.
Chunking	In cognitive psychology and mnemonics, chunking refers to a strategy for making more efficient use of short-term memory by recoding information.
Hypothesis	A specific statement about behavior or mental processes that is testable through research is a hypothesis.
Habit	A habit is a response that has become completely separated from its eliciting stimulus.

	Early learning theorists used the term to describe S-R associations, however not all S-R associations become a habit, rather many are extinguished after reinforcement is withdrawn.
Neuroscience	A field that combines the work of psychologists, biologists, biochemists, medical researchers, and others in the study of the structure and function of the nervous system is neuroscience.
Evolutionary perspective	A perspective that focuses on how humans have evolved and adapted behaviors required for survival against various environmental pressures over the long course is called the evolutionary perspective.
Metaphor	A metaphor is a rhetorical trope where a comparison is made between two seemingly unrelated subjects

Nervous system	The body's electrochemical communication circuitry, made up of billions of neurons is a nervous system.
Analogy	An analogy is a comparison between two different things, in order to highlight some form of similarity. Analogy is the cognitive process of transferring information from a particular subject to another particular subject.
Zygote	A zygote is a cell that is the result of fertilization. That is, two haploid cells—usually (but not always) a sperm cell from a male and an ovum from a female—merge into a single diploid cell called the zygote.
Ovum	Ovum is a female sex cell or gamete.
Deprivation	Deprivation, is the loss or withholding of normal stimulation, nutrition, comfort, love, and so forth; a condition of lacking. The level of stimulation is less than what is required.
Neuron	The neuron is the primary cell of the nervous system. They are found in the brain, the spinal cord, in the nerves and ganglia of the peripheral nervous system. It is a specialized cell that conducts impulses through the nervous system and contains three major parts: cell body, dendrites, and an axon. It can have many dendrites but only one axon.
Glial	Glial cells are non-neuronal cells that provide support and nutrition, maintain homeostasis, form myelin, and participate in signal transmission in the nervous system.
Embryo	A developed zygote that has a rudimentary heart, brain, and other organs is referred to as an embryo.
Mesoderm	The mesoderm is one of the three germ layers in the early developing embryo. The mesoderm gives rise to tissues including connective tissue, muscles and the circulatory system.
Endoderm	The endoderm is one of the three germ layers of the developing embryo, the other two being the ectoderm and the mesoderm. The endoderm gives rise to various tissues including the gastrointestinal tract, respiratory tract, and endocrine glands.
Ectoderm	Ectoderm refers to the outermost cell layer of the newly formed embryo, from which the skin and nervous systems develop.
Protein	A protein is a complex, high-molecular-weight organic compound that consists of amino acids joined by peptide bonds. It is essential to the structure and function of all living cells and viruses. Many are enzymes or subunits of enzymes.
Stem cells	Stem cells are primal undifferentiated cells which retain the ability to differentiate into other cell types. This ability allows them to act as a repair system for the body, replenishing other cells as long as the organism is alive.
Neural tube	The neural tube is the embryonal structure that gives rise to the brain and spinal cord.
Species	Species refers to a reproductively isolated breeding population.
Brain	The brain controls and coordinates most movement, behavior and homeostatic body functions such as heartbeat, blood pressure, fluid balance and body temperature. Functions of the brain are responsible for cognition, emotion, memory, motor learning and other sorts of learning. The brain is primarily made up of two types of cells: glia and neurons.
Dendrite	A dendrite is a slender, typically branched projection of a nerve cell, or "neuron," which conducts the electrical stimulation received from other cells to the body or soma of the cell from which it projects. This stimulation arrives through synapses, which typically are located near the tips of the dendrites and away from the soma.
Axon	An axon, or "nerve fiber," is a long slender projection of a nerve cell, or "neuron," which conducts electrical impulses away from the neuron's cell body or soma.

Interneurons	Interneurons are the neurons that provide connections between sensory and motor neurons, as well as between themselves.
Interneuron	An interneuron (also called relay neuron or association neuron) is a neuron that communicates only to other neurons.
Peripheral nervous system	The peripheral nervous system consists of the nerves and neurons that serve the limbs and organs. It is not protected by bone or the blood-brain barrier, leaving it exposed to toxins and mechanical injuries. The peripheral nervous system is divided into the somatic nervous system and the autonomic nervous system.
Soma	The soma, or cell body, is the bulbous end of a neuron, containing the nucleus. The cell nucleus is a key feature of the soma. The nucleus is the source of most of the RNA that is produced in neurons and most proteins are produced from mRNAs that do not travel far from the nucleus.
Synapse	A synapse is specialized junction through which cells of the nervous system signal to one another and to non-neuronal cells such as muscles or glands.
Sperry	Sperry separated the corpus callosum, the area of the brain used to transfer signals between the right and left hemispheres, to treat epileptics. He then tested these patients with tasks that were known to be dependant on specific hemispheres of the brain and demonstrated that the two halves of the brain now had independent functions.
Cones	Cones are photoreceptors that transmit sensations of color, function in bright light, and used in visual acutity. Infants prior to months of age can only distinguish green and red indicating the cones are not fully developed; they can see all of the colors by 2 months of
Optic nerve	The optic nerve is the nerve that transmits visual information from the retina to the brain. The optic nerve is composed of retinal ganglion cell axons and support cells.
Nerve	A nerve is an enclosed, cable-like bundle of nerve fibers or axons, which includes the glia that ensheath the axons in myelin. Neurons are sometimes called nerve cells, though this term is technically imprecise since many neurons do not form nerves.
Hypothesis	A specific statement about behavior or mental processes that is testable through research is a hypothesis.
Comparative research	Comparative research is a research methodology that aims to make comparisons across different countries or cultures. A major problem is that the data sets in different countries may not use the same categories, or define categories differently.
Ganglion cell	A ganglion cell is a type of neuron located in the retina of the eye that receives visual information from photoreceptors via various intermediate cells such as bipolar cells, amacrine cells, and horizontal cells. Retinal ganglion cells' axons are myelinated.
Ganglion	A ganglion is a tissue mass that contains the dendrites and cell bodies (or "somas") of nerve cells, in most case ones belonging to the peripheral nervous system. Within the central nervous system such a mass is often called a nucleus.
Retina	The retina is a thin layer of cells at the back of the eyeball. It is the part of the eye which converts light into nervous signals. The retina contains photoreceptor cells which receive the light; the resulting neural signals then undergo complex processing by other neurons of the retina, and are transformed into action potentials in retinal ganglion cells whose axons form the optic nerve.
Projection	Attributing one's own undesirable thoughts, impulses, traits, or behaviors to others is referred to as projection.
Neurotransmitter	A neurotransmitter is a chemical that is used to relay, amplify and modulate electrical

signals between a neurons and another cell.

Spinal cord | The spinal cord is a part of the vertebrate nervous system that is enclosed in and protected by the vertebral column (it passes through the spinal canal). It consists of nerve cells. The spinal cord carries sensory signals and motor innervation to most of the skeletal muscles in the body.

Astrocyte | An astrocyte, also known as astroglia, is a characteristic star-shaped cell in the brain. They are the biggest cells found in brain tissue and outnumber the neurons ten to one. A commonly accepted function is to structure physically the brain. A second function is to provide neurons with nutrients such as glucose. They regulate the flow of nutrients provided by capillaries by forming the blood-brain barrier.

In vitro | In vitro is an experimental technique where the experiment is performed in a test tube, or generally outside a living organism or cell.

Apoptosis | Apoptosis is one of the main types of programmed cell death. As such, it is a process of deliberate suicide by an unwanted cell in a multicellular organism.

Necrosis | Necrosis is the name given to unprogrammed death of cells/living tissue. There are many causes of necrosis including injury, infection, cancer, infarction, and inflammation.

Axon terminal | A swelling at the end of an axon that is designed to release a chemical substance onto another neuron, muscle cell, or gland cell is called the axon terminal.

Stages | Stages represent relatively discrete periods of time in which functioning is qualitatively different from functioning at other periods.

Postnatal | Postnatal is the period beginning immediately after the birth of a child and extending for about six weeks. The period is also known as postpartum and, less commonly, puerperium.

Prefrontal cortex | The prefrontal cortex is the anterior part of the frontal lobes of the brain, lying in front of the motor and associative areas. It has been implicated in planning complex cognitive behaviors, personality expression and moderating correct social behavior. The prefrontal cortex continues to develop until around age 6.

Olfactory bulb | The olfactory bulb is a part of the brain that is a distinct outgrowth from the forebrain. It plays a major role in olfaction, which is the perception of smells. The olfactory bulb receives direct input from olfactory nerve, made up of the axons from approximately 10 million olfactory receptor neurons in the olfactory mucosa, a region of the nasal cavity.

Hippocampus | The hippocampus is a part of the brain located inside the temporal lobe. It forms a part of the limbic system and plays a part in memory and navigation.

Prenatal | Prenatal period refers to the time from conception to birth.

Myelination | The process in which the nerve cells are covered and insulated with a layer of fat cells, which increases the speed at which information travels through the nervous system is referred to as myelination.

Adolescence | The period of life bounded by puberty and the assumption of adult responsibilities is adolescence.

Synaptic density | Synaptic density is believed to be an important indication of the extent of connectivity between neurons.

Plasticity | The capacity for modification and change is referred to as plasticity.

Cognitive development | The process by which a child's understanding of the world changes as a function of age and experience is called cognitive development.

Working Memory | Working memory is the collection of structures and processes in the brain used for

	temporarily storing and manipulating information. Working memory consists of both memory for items that are currently being processed, and components governing attention and directing the processing itself.
Piaget	Piaget argued that young children's answers were qualitatively different than older children rather than quantitative. There are two major aspects to his theory: the process of coming to know and the stages we move through as we gradually acquire this ability.
Perseveration	The persistent repetition of words and ideas, often found in schizophrenia is called perseveration.
Lesion	A lesion is a non-specific term referring to abnormal tissue in the body. It can be caused by any disease process including trauma (physical, chemical, electrical), infection, neoplasm, metabolic and autoimmune.
Visual cortex	The visual cortex is the general term applied to both the primary visual cortex and the visual association area. Anatomically, the visual cortex occupies the entire occipital lobe, the inferior temporal lobe (IT), posterior parts of the parietal lobe, and a few small regions in the frontal lobe.
Monocular	Depth perception combines several types of depth clues grouped into two categories: monocular clues, available from the input of just one eye, and binocular clues. Monocular clues include motion parallax, color vision, perspective, relative size, distance fog, depth from focus, and occlusion
Primary visual cortex	Primary visual cortex refers to the area at the rear of the occipital lobes where vision registers in the cerebral cortex.
Nucleus	In neuroanatomy, a cluster of cell bodies of neurons within the central nervous system is a nucleus.
Lateral geniculate nucleus	The lateral geniculate nucleus of the thalamus is a part of the brain, which is the primary processor of visual information, received from the retina, in the CNS.
Sensitive period	A sensitive period is a developmental window in which a predisposed behavior is most likely to develop given appropriate stimulation. In linguistic theory, the period from about 18 months to puberty is when the brain is thought to be primed for learning language because of plasticity of the brain.
Motor neuron	A motor neuron is an efferent neuron that originates in the spinal cord and synapses with muscle fibers to facilitate muscle contraction and with muscle spindles to modify proprioceptive sensitivity.
Neurogenesis	Neurogenesis literally means "birth of neurons". Neurogenesis is most prevalent during pre-natal development and is the process by which neurons are created to populate the growing brain.
Association cortex	Region of the cerebral cortex in which the highest intellectual functions, including thinking and problem solving, occur is the association cortex.
Gyrus	A gyrus is a ridge on the cerebral cortex. It is generally surrounded by one or more sulci.
Motor cortex	Motor cortex refers to the section of cortex that lies in the frontal lobe, just across the central fissure from the sensory cortex. Neural impulses in the motor cortex are linked to muscular responses throughout the body.
Somatosensory	Somatosensory system consists of the various sensory receptors that trigger the experiences labelled as touch or pressure, temperature, pain, and the sensations of muscle movement and joint position including posture, movement, and facial expression.

Somatosensory cortex	The primary somatosensory cortex is across the central sulcus and behind the primary motor cortex configured to generally correspond with the arrangement of nearby motor cells related to specific body parts. It is the main sensory receptive area for the sense of touch.
Autism	Autism is a neurodevelopmental disorder that manifests itself in markedly abnormal social interaction, communication ability, patterns of interests, and patterns of behavior.
Emotion	An emotion is a mental states that arise spontaneously, rather than through conscious effort. They are often accompanied by physiological changes.
Sears	Sears focused on the application of the social learning theory (SLT) to socialization processes, and how children internalize the values, attitudes, and behaviors predominant in their culture. He articulated the place of parents in fostering internalization. In addition, he was among the first social learning theorists to officially acknowledge the reciprocal interaction on an individual's behavior and their environment
Behavioral therapy	The treatment of a mental disorder through the application of basic principles of conditioning and learning is called behavioral therapy.
Heterogeneous	A heterogeneous compound, mixture, or other such object is one that consists of many different items, which are often not easily sorted or separated, though they are clearly distinct.
Pitch	Pitch is the psychological interpretation of a sound or musical tone corresponding to its physical frequency
Social skills	Social skills are skills used to interact and communicate with others to assist status in the social structure and other motivations.
Population	Population refers to all members of a well-defined group of organisms, events, or things.
Syndrome	The term syndrome is the association of several clinically recognizable features, signs, symptoms, phenomena or characteristics which often occur together, so that the presence of one feature indicates the presence of the others.
Gene	A gene is an ultramicroscopic area of the chromosome. It is the smallest physical unit of the DNA molecule that carries a piece of hereditary information.
Chromosome	The DNA which carries genetic information in biological cells is normally packaged in the form of one or more large macromolecules called a chromosome. Humans normally have 46.
Etiology	Etiology is the study of causation. The term is used in philosophy, physics and biology in reference to the causes of various phenomena. It is generally the study of why things occur, or even the reasons behind the way that things act.
Limbic system	The limbic system is a group of brain structures that are involved in various emotions such as aggression, fear, pleasure and also in the formation of memory. The limbic system affects the endocrine system and the autonomic nervous system. It consists of several subcortical structures located around the thalamus.
Evolutionary perspective	A perspective that focuses on how humans have evolved and adapted behaviors required for survival against various environmental pressures over the long course is called the evolutionary perspective.
Animal model	An animal model usually refers to a non-human animal with a disease that is similar to a human condition.

Brain | The brain controls and coordinates most movement, behavior and homeostatic body functions such as heartbeat, blood pressure, fluid balance and body temperature. Functions of the brain are responsible for cognition, emotion, memory, motor learning and other sorts of learning. The brain is primarily made up of two types of cells: glia and neurons.

Cranial nerve | A Cranial nerve emerges from the brainstem instead of the spinal cord.

Neurologist | A physician who studies the nervous system, especially its structure, functions, and abnormalities is referred to as neurologist.

Tumor | A tumor is an abnormal growth that when located in the brain can either be malignant and directly destroy brain tissue, or be benign and disrupt functioning by increasing intracranial pressure.

Nerve | A nerve is an enclosed, cable-like bundle of nerve fibers or axons, which includes the glia that ensheath the axons in myelin. Neurons are sometimes called nerve cells, though this term is technically imprecise since many neurons do not form nerves.

Morphine | Morphine, the principal active agent in opium, is a powerful opioid analgesic drug. According to recent research, it may also be produced naturally by the human brain. Morphine is usually highly addictive, and tolerance and physical and psychological dependence develop quickly.

Programmed cell death | Programmed cell death is the deliberate suicide of an unwanted cell in a multicellular organism.

Wechsler | Wechsler is best known for his intelligence tests. The Wechsler Adult Intelligence Scale (WAIS) was developed first in 1939 and then called the Wechsler-Bellevue Intelligence Test. From these he derived the Wechsler Intelligence Scale for Children (WISC) in 1949 and the Wechsler Preschool and Primary Scale of Intelligence (WPPSI) in 1967. Wechsler originally created these tests to find out more about his patients at the Bellevue clinic and he found the then-current Binet IQ test unsatisfactory.

Nervous system | The body's electrochemical communication circuitry, made up of billions of neurons is a nervous system.

Meninges | The meninges are the system of membranes that envelop the central nervous system. The meninges consist of three layers, the dura mater, the arachnoid mater, and the pia mater.

Central nervous system | The vertebrate central nervous system consists of the brain and spinal cord.

Lungs | The lungs are the essential organs of respiration. Its principal function is to transport oxygen from the atmosphere into the bloodstream, and excrete carbon dioxide from the bloodstream into the atmosphere.

Stroke | A stroke occurs when the blood supply to a part of the brain is suddenly interrupted by occlusion, by hemorrhage, or other causes

Ischemia | Narrowing of arteries caused by plaque buildup within the arteries is called ischemia.

Amnesia | Amnesia is a condition in which memory is disturbed. The causes of amnesia are organic or functional. Organic causes include damage to the brain, through trauma or disease, or use of certain (generally sedative) drugs.

Aphasia | Aphasia is a loss or impairment of the ability to produce or comprehend language, due to brain damage. It is usually a result of damage to the language centers of the brain.

Cerebral hemorrhage | Cerebral hemorrhage is a form of stroke that occurs when a blood vessel in the brain ruptures or bleeds. Hemorrhagic strokes are deadlier than their more common counterpart, ischemic strokes.

Congenital	A condition existing at birth is referred to as congenital.
Thrombosis	Thrombosis is the formation of a clot inside a blood vessel, obstructing the flow of blood through the circulatory system. A cerebral thrombosis can result in stroke.
Amino acid	Amino acid is the basic structural building unit of proteins. They form short polymer chains called peptides or polypeptides which in turn form structures called proteins.
Glutamate	Glutamate is one of the 20 standard amino acids used by all organisms in their proteins. It is critical for proper cell function, but it is not an essential nutrient in humans because it can be manufactured from other compounds.
Neurotransmitter	A neurotransmitter is a chemical that is used to relay, amplify and modulate electrical signals between a neurons and another cell.
Receptor	A sensory receptor is a structure that recognizes a stimulus in the internal or external environment of an organism. In response to stimuli the sensory receptor initiates sensory transduction by creating graded potentials or action potentials in the same cell or in an adjacent one.
Neuron	The neuron is the primary cell of the nervous system. They are found in the brain, the spinal cord, in the nerves and ganglia of the peripheral nervous system. It is a specialized cell that conducts impulses through the nervous system and contains three major parts: cell body, dendrites, and an axon. It can have many dendrites but only one axon.
Affect	A subjective feeling or emotional tone often accompanied by bodily expressions noticeable to others is called affect.
Ion	An ion is an atom or group of atoms with a net electric charge. The energy required to detach an electron in its lowest energy state from an atom or molecule of a gas with less net electric charge is called the ionization potential, or ionization energy.
Blocking	If the one of the two members of a compound stimulus fails to produce the CR due to an earlier conditioning of the other member of the compound stimulus, blocking has occurred.
Contusion	Brain contusion, a form of traumatic brain injury, is a bruise of the brain tissue. Like bruises in other tissues, cerebral contusion can be caused by multiple microhemorrhages, small blood vessel leaks into brain tissue.
Paradoxical	Paradoxical intention refers to instructing clients to do the opposite of the desired behavior. Telling an impotent man not to have sex or an insomniac not to sleep reduces anxiety to perform.
Dura mater	The dura mater is the tough and inflexible outermost of the three layers of the meninges surrounding the brain. The other two meninges are the pia mater and the arachnoid mater. The dura mater envelops and protects the brain and spinal cord.
Consciousness	The awareness of the sensations, thoughts, and feelings being experienced at a given moment is called consciousness.
Concussion	Concussion, or mild traumatic brain injury (MTBI), is the most common and least serious type of brain injury. A milder type of diffuse axonal injury, concussion involves a transient loss of mental function. It can be caused by acceleration or deceleration forces, by a direct blow, or by penetrating injuries.
Dementia	Dementia is progressive decline in cognitive function due to damage or disease in the brain beyond what might be expected from normal aging.
Syndrome	The term syndrome is the association of several clinically recognizable features, signs, symptoms, phenomena or characteristics which often occur together, so that the presence of one feature indicates the presence of the others.

Encephalitis	Encephalitis is an acute inflammation of the brain, commonly caused by a viral infection.
Syphilis	Syphilis is a sexually transmitted disease that is caused by a spirochaete bacterium, Treponema pallidum. If not treated, syphilis can cause serious effects such as damage to the nervous system, heart, or brain. Untreated syphilis can be ultimately fatal.
Insanity	A legal status indicating that a person cannot be held responsible for his or her actions because of mental illness is called insanity.
Gastrointestinal tract	The gastrointestinal tract is the system of organs within multicellular animals which takes in food, digests it to extract energy and nutrients, and expels the remaining waste.
Mercury	Elemental, liquid mercury is slightly toxic, while its vapor, compounds and salts are highly toxic and have been implicated as causing brain and liver damage when ingested, inhaled or contacted. Because mercury is easily transferred across the placenta, the embryo is highly susceptible to birth defects.
Psychosis	Psychosis is a generic term for mental states in which the components of rational thought and perception are severely impaired. Persons experiencing a psychosis may experience hallucinations, hold paranoid or delusional beliefs, demonstrate personality changes and exhibit disorganized thinking. This is usually accompanied by features such as a lack of insight into the unusual or bizarre nature of their behavior, difficulties with social interaction and impairments in carrying out the activities of daily living.
Antipsychotic	The term antipsychotic is applied to a group of drugs used to treat psychosis.
Chromosome	The DNA which carries genetic information in biological cells is normally packaged in the form of one or more large macromolecules called a chromosome. Humans normally have 46.
Antibody	An antibody is a protein used by the immune system to identify and neutralize foreign objects like bacteria and viruses. Each antibody recognizes a specific antigen unique to its target.
Recessive gene	Recessive gene refers to an allele that causes a phenotype (visible or detectable characteristic) that is only seen in a homozygous genotype (an organism that has two copies of the same allele). Thus, both parents have to be carriers of a recessive trait in order for a child to express that trait.
Gene	A gene is an ultramicroscopic area of the chromosome. It is the smallest physical unit of the DNA molecule that carries a piece of hereditary information.
Dominant gene	In genetics, the term dominant gene refers to the allele that causes a phenotype that is seen in a heterozygous genotype.
Puberty	Puberty refers to the process of physical changes by which a child's body becomes an adult body capable of reproduction.
Down syndrome	Down syndrome encompasses a number of genetic disorders, of which trisomy 21 (a nondisjunction, the so-called extrachromosone) is the most representative, causing highly variable degrees of learning difficulties as well as physical disabilities. Incidence of Down syndrome is estimated at 1 per 660 births, making it the most common chromosomal abnormality.
Genetic disorder	A genetic disorder is a disease caused by abnormal expression of one or more genes in a person causing a clinical phenotype.
Ovulation	Ovulation is the process in the menstrual cycle by which a mature ovarian follicle ruptures and discharges an ovum (also known as an oocyte, female gamete, or casually, an egg) that participates in reproduction.
Zygote	A zygote is a cell that is the result of fertilization. That is, two haploid cells—usually (but not always) a sperm cell from a male and an ovum from a female—merge into a single diploid cell called the zygote.

Protein	A protein is a complex, high-molecular-weight organic compound that consists of amino acids joined by peptide bonds. It is essential to the structure and function of all living cells and viruses. Many are enzymes or subunits of enzymes.
Apoptosis	Apoptosis is one of the main types of programmed cell death. As such, it is a process of deliberate suicide by an unwanted cell in a multicellular organism.
Suicide	Suicide behavior is rare in childhood but escalates in adolescence. The suicide rate increases in a linear fashion from adolescence through late adulthood.
Necrosis	Necrosis is the name given to unprogrammed death of cells/living tissue. There are many causes of necrosis including injury, infection, cancer, infarction, and inflammation.
Dendrite	A dendrite is a slender, typically branched projection of a nerve cell, or "neuron," which conducts the electrical stimulation received from other cells to the body or soma of the cell from which it projects. This stimulation arrives through synapses, which typically are located near the tips of the dendrites and away from the soma.
Axon	An axon, or "nerve fiber," is a long slender projection of a nerve cell, or "neuron," which conducts electrical impulses away from the neuron's cell body or soma.
Epilepsy	Epilepsy is a chronic neurological condition characterized by recurrent unprovoked neural discharges. It is commonly controlled with medication, although surgical methods are used as well.
Seizure	A seizure is a temporary alteration in brain function expressed as a changed mental state, tonic or clonic movements and various other symptoms. They are due to temporary abnormal electrical activity of a group of brain cells.
Chronic	Chronic refers to a relatively long duration, usually more than a few months.
Population	Population refers to all members of a well-defined group of organisms, events, or things.
Electroencep-alogram	Electroencephalography is the neurophysiologic measurement of the electrical activity of the brain by recording from electrodes placed on the scalp, or in the special cases on the cortex. The resulting traces are known as an electroencephalogram and represent so-called brainwaves.
Electrode	Any device used to electrically stimulate nerve tissue or to record its activity is an electrode.
Lobes	The four major sections of the cerebral cortex: frontal, parietal, temporal, and occipital are called lobes.
Temporal lobe	The temporal lobe is part of the cerebrum. It lies at the side of the brain, beneath the lateral or Sylvian fissure. Adjacent areas in the superior, posterior and lateral parts of the temporal lobe are involved in high-level auditory processing.
Senses	The senses are systems that consist of a sensory cell type that respond to a specific kind of physical energy, and that correspond to a defined region within the brain where the signals are received and interpreted.
Hypoxia	Hypoxia is a pathological condition in which the body as a whole or region of the body is deprived of adequate oxygen supply.
Dopamine	Dopamine is critical to the way the brain controls our movements and is a crucial part of the basal ganglia motor loop. It is commonly associated with the 'pleasure system' of the brain, providing feelings of enjoyment and reinforcement to motivate us to do, or continue doing, certain activities.
Substantia nigra	The substantia nigra is a portion of the midbrain thought to be involved in certain aspects

	of movement and attention. Degeneration of cells in this region is the principle pathology that underlies Parkinson's disease.
Agonist	Agonist refers to a drug that mimics or increases a neurotransmitter's effects.
Mutation	Mutation is a permanent, sometimes transmissible (if the change is to a germ cell) change to the genetic material (usually DNA or RNA) of a cell. They can be caused by copying errors in the genetic material during cell division and by exposure to radiation, chemicals, or viruses, or can occur deliberately under cellular control during the processes such as meiosis or hypermutation.
Tremor	Tremor is the rhythmic, oscillating shaking movement of the whole body or just a certain part of it, caused by problems of the neurons responsible from muscle action.
Depression	In everyday language depression refers to any downturn in mood, which may be relatively transitory and perhaps due to something trivial. This is differentiated from Clinical depression which is marked by symptoms that last two weeks or more and are so severe that they interfere with daily living.
Basal ganglia	The basal ganglia are a group of nuclei in the brain associated with motor and learning functions.
Midbrain	Located between the hindbrain and forebrain, a region in which many nerve-fiber systems ascend and descend to connect the higher and lower portions of the brain is referred to as midbrain. It is archipallian in origin, meaning its general architecture is shared with the most ancient of vertebrates. Dopamine produced in the subtantia nigra plays a role in motivation and habituation of species from humans to the most elementary animals such as insects.
Nucleus	In neuroanatomy, a cluster of cell bodies of neurons within the central nervous system is a nucleus.
Traumatic brain injury	Traumatic brain injury, also called acquired brain injury, intracranial injury, or simply head injury, occurs when a sudden trauma causes damage to the brain.
Nigrostriatal pathway	The nigrostriatal pathway is a neural pathway which connects the substantia nigra with the striatum. It is one of the major dopamine pathways in the brain, and is particularly involved in the production of movement, as part of a system called the basal ganglia motor loop.
Myelin	Myelin is an electrically insulating fatty layer that surrounds the axons of many neurons, especially those in the peripheral nervous system. The main consequence of a myelin sheath is an increase in the speed at which impulses propagate along the myelinated fiber. The sheath continues to develop throughout childhood.
Multiple sclerosis	Multiple sclerosis affects neurons, the cells of the brain and spinal cord that carry information, create thought and perception, and allow the brain to control the body. Surrounding and protecting these neurons is a layer of fat, called myelin, which helps neurons carry electrical signals. MS causes gradual destruction of myelin (demyelination) in patches throughout the brain and/or spinal cord, causing various symptoms depending upon which signals are interrupted.
Lesion	A lesion is a non-specific term referring to abnormal tissue in the body. It can be caused by any disease process including trauma (physical, chemical, electrical), infection, neoplasm, metabolic and autoimmune.
Ataxia	Ataxia is unsteady and clumsy motion of the limbs or trunk due to a failure of the fine coordination of muscle movements.
Epidemiology	Epidemiology is the study of the distribution and determinants of disease and disorders in human populations, and the use of its knowledge to control health problems.Epidemiology is

	considered the cornerstone methodology in all of public health research, and is highly regarded in evidence-based clinical medicine for identifying risk factors for disease and determining optimal treatment approaches to clinical practice.
Predisposition	Predisposition refers to an inclination or diathesis to respond in a certain way, either inborn or acquired. In abnormal psychology, it is a factor that lowers the ability to withstand stress and inclines the individual toward pathology.
Immune system	The most important function of the human immune system occurs at the cellular level of the blood and tissues. The lymphatic and blood circulation systems are highways for specialized white blood cells. These cells include B cells, T cells, natural killer cells, and macrophages. All function with the primary objective of recognizing, attacking and destroying bacteria, viruses, cancer cells, and all substances seen as foreign.
Animal model	An animal model usually refers to a non-human animal with a disease that is similar to a human condition.
Stages	Stages represent relatively discrete periods of time in which functioning is qualitatively different from functioning at other periods.
Tangles	Tangles are twisted fibers that build up inside nerve cells.
Plaques	Plaques refer to small, round areas composed of remnants of lost neurons and beta-amyloid, a waxy protein deposit; present in the brains of patients with Alzheimer's disease.
Neurofibrillary tangles	Neurofibrillary tangles are pathological protein aggregates found within neurons in cases of Alzheimer's disease.
Cytoplasm	Cytoplasm is the colloidal, semi-fluid matter contained within the cell's plasma membrane, in which organelles are suspended. In contrast to the protoplasm, the cytoplasm does not include the cell nucleus, the interior of which is made up of nucleoplasm.
Genetics	Genetics is the science of genes, heredity, and the variation of organisms.
Amygdala	Located in the brain's medial temporal lobe, the almond-shaped amygdala is believed to play a key role in the emotions. It forms part of the limbic system and is linked to both fear responses and pleasure. Its size is positively correlated with aggressive behavior across species.
Prefrontal cortex	The prefrontal cortex is the anterior part of the frontal lobes of the brain, lying in front of the motor and associative areas. It has been implicated in planning complex cognitive behaviors, personality expression and moderating correct social behavior. The prefrontal cortex continues to develop until around age 6.
Hypothesis	A specific statement about behavior or mental processes that is testable through research is a hypothesis.
Modeling	A type of behavior learned through observation of others demonstrating the same behavior is modeling.
Goddard	Goddard is known especially for his 1912 work, The Kallikak Family: A Study in the Heredity of Feeble-Mindedness and for being the first to translate the Binet intelligence test into English in 1908.
Emotion	An emotion is a mental states that arise spontaneously, rather than through conscious effort. They are often accompanied by physiological changes.
Pinel	Pinel is regarded as the father of modern psychiatry. He was a clinician believing that medical truth derived from clinical experience. While at Bicêtre, Pinel did away with bleeding, purging, and blistering in favor a therapy that involved close contact with and careful observation of patients.

Species	Species refers to a reproductively isolated breeding population.
Bradykinesia	Bradykinesia denotes "slow movement." It is a feature of a number of diseases, most notably Parkinson's disease and other disorders of the basal ganglia.
Heroin	Heroin is widely and illegally used as a powerful and addictive drug producing intense euphoria, which often disappears with increasing tolerance. Heroin is a semi-synthetic opioid. It is the 3,6-diacetyl derivative of morphine and is synthesised from it by acetylation.
Distal	Students can set both long-term (distal) and short-term (proximal) goals .
Synapse	A synapse is specialized junction through which cells of the nervous system signal to one another and to non-neuronal cells such as muscles or glands.
Schwann cell	A Schwann cell is a variety of neuroglia that wraps around axons in the peripheral nervous system, forming the myelin sheath. The nervous system depends crucially on this sheath for insulation and an increase in impulse speed.
Cell membrane	A component of every biological cell, the selectively permeable cell membrane is a thin and structured bilayer of phospholipid and protein molecules that envelopes the cell. It separates a cell's interior from its surroundings and controls what moves in and out.
Axon terminal	A swelling at the end of an axon that is designed to release a chemical substance onto another neuron, muscle cell, or gland cell is called the axon terminal.
Nodes of Ranvier	Nodes of Ranvier are regularly spaced gaps in the myelin sheath around an axon or nerve fiber. About one micrometer in length, these gaps expose the membrane of the axon to the surrounding liquid. Ion flow occurs only at the nodes of Ranvier.
Learning	Learning is a relatively permanent change in behavior that results from experience. Thus, to attribute a behavioral change to learning, the change must be relatively permanent and must result from experience.
Motor neuron	A motor neuron is an efferent neuron that originates in the spinal cord and synapses with muscle fibers to facilitate muscle contraction and with muscle spindles to modify proprioceptive sensitivity.
Motor cortex	Motor cortex refers to the section of cortex that lies in the frontal lobe, just across the central fissure from the sensory cortex. Neural impulses in the motor cortex are linked to muscular responses throughout the body.
Retina	The retina is a thin layer of cells at the back of the eyeball. It is the part of the eye which converts light into nervous signals. The retina contains photoreceptor cells which receive the light; the resulting neural signals then undergo complex processing by other neurons of the retina, and are transformed into action potentials in retinal ganglion cells whose axons form the optic nerve.
Receptive field	The receptive field of a sensory neuron is a region of sensitivity in which the presence of a stimulus will alter the firing of that neuron.
Sensory neuron	A sensory neuron is an afferent nerve cell within the nervous system responsible for converting external stimuli from the organism's environment into internal electrical impulses. It carries messages from a sensory organ, through a nerve, into the brain or spinal cord.
Visual cortex	The visual cortex is the general term applied to both the primary visual cortex and the visual association area. Anatomically, the visual cortex occupies the entire occipital lobe, the inferior temporal lobe (IT), posterior parts of the parietal lobe, and a few small regions in the frontal lobe.

Somatosensory | Somatosensory system consists of the various sensory receptors that trigger the experiences labelled as touch or pressure, temperature, pain, and the sensations of muscle movement and joint position including posture, movement, and facial expression.

Pons | The pons is a knob on the brain stem. It is part of the autonomic nervous system, and relays sensory information between the cerebellum and cerebrum. Some theories posit that it has a role in dreaming.

Primary visual cortex | Primary visual cortex refers to the area at the rear of the occipital lobes where vision registers in the cerebral cortex.

Somatosensory cortex | The primary somatosensory cortex is across the central sulcus and behind the primary motor cortex configured to generally correspond with the arrangement of nearby motor cells related to specific body parts. It is the main sensory receptive area for the sense of touch.

Neurogenesis | Neurogenesis literally means "birth of neurons". Neurogenesis is most prevalent during pre-natal development and is the process by which neurons are created to populate the growing brain.

Hippocampus | The hippocampus is a part of the brain located inside the temporal lobe. It forms a part of the limbic system and plays a part in memory and navigation.

Gyrus | A gyrus is a ridge on the cerebral cortex. It is generally surrounded by one or more sulci.

Neuroscience | A field that combines the work of psychologists, biologists, biochemists, medical researchers, and others in the study of the structure and function of the nervous system is neuroscience.

Maturation | The orderly unfolding of traits, as regulated by the genetic code is called maturation.

Estrogen | Estrogen is a group of steroid compounds that function as the primary female sex hormone. They are produced primarily by developing follicles in the ovaries, the corpus luteum and the placenta.

Hormone | A hormone is a chemical messenger from one cell (or group of cells) to another. The best known are those produced by endocrine glands, but they are produced by nearly every organ system. The function of hormones is to serve as a signal to the target cells; the action of the hormone is determined by the pattern of secretion and the signal transduction of the receiving tissue.

Steroid | A steroid is a lipid characterized by a carbon skeleton with four fused rings. Different steroids vary in the functional groups attached to these rings. Hundreds of distinct steroids have been identified in plants and animals. Their most important role in most living systems is as hormones.

Gonads | The gonads are the organs that make gametes. Gametes are haploid germ cells. For example, sperm and egg cells are gametes. In the male the gonads are the testicles, and in the female the gonads are the ovaries.

Ovary | The female reproductive organ is the ovary. It performs two major functions: producing eggs and secreting hormones.

Optic nerve | The optic nerve is the nerve that transmits visual information from the retina to the brain. The optic nerve is composed of retinal ganglion cell axons and support cells.

Ganglion cell | A ganglion cell is a type of neuron located in the retina of the eye that receives visual information from photoreceptors via various intermediate cells such as bipolar cells, amacrine cells, and horizontal cells. Retinal ganglion cells' axons are myelinated.

Ganglion | A ganglion is a tissue mass that contains the dendrites and cell bodies (or "somas") of nerve cells, in most case ones belonging to the peripheral nervous system. Within the central

	nervous system such a mass is often called a nucleus.
Oligodendrocyte	An Oligodendrocyte is a variety of neuroglia. Their main function is the myelination of nerve cells exclusively in the central nervous system of the higher vertebrates. A single oligodendrocyte can extend to about a dozen axons, wrapping around approximately 1mm of each and forming the myelin sheath.
Spinal cord	The spinal cord is a part of the vertebrate nervous system that is enclosed in and protected by the vertebral column (it passes through the spinal canal). It consists of nerve cells. The spinal cord carries sensory signals and motor innervation to most of the skeletal muscles in the body.
Olfactory bulb	The olfactory bulb is a part of the brain that is a distinct outgrowth from the forebrain. It plays a major role in olfaction, which is the perception of smells. The olfactory bulb receives direct input from olfactory nerve, made up of the axons from approximately 10 million olfactory receptor neurons in the olfactory mucosa, a region of the nasal cavity.
Olfactory system	The olfactory system is the sensory system used for the sense of smell. The olfactory system is often spoken of along with the gustatory system as the chemosensory senses because both transduce chemical signals into perception
Stem cells	Stem cells are primal undifferentiated cells which retain the ability to differentiate into other cell types. This ability allows them to act as a repair system for the body, replenishing other cells as long as the organism is alive.
Case study	A carefully drawn biography that may be obtained through interviews, questionnaires, and psychological tests is called a case study.
Placebo	Placebo refers to a bogus treatment that has the appearance of being genuine.
Attention	Attention is the cognitive process of selectively concentrating on one thing while ignoring other things. Psychologists have labeled three types of attention: sustained attention, selective attention, and divided attention.
Feedback	Feedback refers to information returned to a person about the effects a response has had.
Phantom limb	Phantom limb is a feeling that a missing limb is still attached to the body and is moving appropriately with other body parts. Phantom pains can also occur in people who are born without limbs and people who are paralyzed.
Premise	A premise is a statement presumed true within the context of a discourse, especially of a logical argument.
Neuropsychologist	A psychologist concerned with the relationships among cognition, affect, behavior, and brain function is a neuropsychologist.
Perception	Perception is the process of acquiring, interpreting, selecting, and organizing sensory information.
Insight	Insight refers to a sudden awareness of the relationships among various elements that had previously appeared to be independent of one another.
Sensation	Sensation is the first stage in the chain of biochemical and neurologic events that begins with the impinging of a stimulus upon the receptor cells of a sensory organ, which then leads to perception, the mental state that is reflected in statements like "I see a uniformly blue wall."
Evolutionary perspective	A perspective that focuses on how humans have evolved and adapted behaviors required for survival against various environmental pressures over the long course is called the evolutionary perspective.

Learning	Learning is a relatively permanent change in behavior that results from experience. Thus, to attribute a behavioral change to learning, the change must be relatively permanent and must result from experience.
Brain	The brain controls and coordinates most movement, behavior and homeostatic body functions such as heartbeat, blood pressure, fluid balance and body temperature. Functions of the brain are responsible for cognition, emotion, memory, motor learning and other sorts of learning. The brain is primarily made up of two types of cells: glia and neurons.
Animal model	An animal model usually refers to a non-human animal with a disease that is similar to a human condition.
Amnesia	Amnesia is a condition in which memory is disturbed. The causes of amnesia are organic or functional. Organic causes include damage to the brain, through trauma or disease, or use of certain (generally sedative) drugs.
Neuropsychology	Neuropsychology is a branch of psychology that aims to understand how the structure and function of the brain relates to specific psychological processes.
Neuropsychol-gist	A psychologist concerned with the relationships among cognition, affect, behavior, and brain function is a neuropsychologist.
Temporal lobe	The temporal lobe is part of the cerebrum. It lies at the side of the brain, beneath the lateral or Sylvian fissure. Adjacent areas in the superior, posterior and lateral parts of the temporal lobe are involved in high-level auditory processing.
Lobes	The four major sections of the cerebral cortex: frontal, parietal, temporal, and occipital are called lobes.
Electroencep-alography	Electroencephalography is the neurophysiologic measurement of the electrical activity of the brain by recording from electrodes placed on the scalp, or in special cases on the cortex. The resulting traces are known as an electroencephalogram (EEG) and represent so-called brainwaves.
Seizure	A seizure is a temporary alteration in brain function expressed as a changed mental state, tonic or clonic movements and various other symptoms. They are due to temporary abnormal electrical activity of a group of brain cells.
Olfactory bulb	The olfactory bulb is a part of the brain that is a distinct outgrowth from the forebrain. It plays a major role in olfaction, which is the perception of smells. The olfactory bulb receives direct input from olfactory nerve, made up of the axons from approximately 10 million olfactory receptor neurons in the olfactory mucosa, a region of the nasal cavity.
Optic chiasm	Optic chiasm refers to the point at which the optic nerves from the inside half of each eye cross over and then project to the opposite half of the brain.
Frontal lobe	The frontal lobe comprises four major folds of cortical tissue: the precentral gyrus, superior gyrus and the middle gyrus of the frontal gyri, the inferior frontal gyrus. It has been found to play a part in impulse control, judgement, language, memory, motor function, problem solving, sexual behavior, socialization and spontaneity.
Anterograde amnesia	Anterograde amnesia is a form of amnesia where new events are not transferred to long-term memory, so the sufferer will not be able to remember anything that occurs after the onset of this type of amnesia for more than a few moments.
Attention	Attention is the cognitive process of selectively concentrating on one thing while ignoring other things. Psychologists have labeled three types of attention: sustained attention, selective attention, and divided attention.
Retention	Retention interval is the time between training and testing in which forgetting may occur.

interval	
Sensorimotor	The first of Piaget's stages is the Sensorimotor stage. This stage typically ranges from birth to 2 years. In this stage, children experience the world through their senses. During this stage, object permanence and stranger anxiety develop.
Conditioning	Conditioning describes the process by which behaviors can be learned or modified through interaction with the environment.
Pavlovian conditioning	Pavlovian conditioning, synonymous with classical conditioning is a type of learning found in animals, caused by the association (or pairing) of two stimuli or what Ivan Pavlov described as the learning of conditional behavior, therefore called conditioning.
Conditioned response	A conditioned response is the response to a stimulus that occurs when an animal has learned to associate the stimulus with a certain positive or negative effect.
Mnemonic	A mnemonic is a memory aid. They are often verbal, are sometimes in verse form, and are often used to remember lists.
Implicit memory	Implicit memory is the long-term memory of skills and procedures, or "how to" knowledge. It is often not easily verbalized, but can be used without consciously thinking about it.
Priming	A phenomenon in which exposure to a word or concept later makes it easier to recall related information, even when one has no conscious memory of the word or concept is called priming.
Control subjects	Control subjects are participants in an experiment who do not receive the treatment effect but for whom all other conditions are held comparable to those of experimental subjects.
Explicit memory	Intentional or conscious recollection of information is referred to as explicit memory. Children under age three are usually poorest at explicit memory which may be due to the immaturity of the prefrontal lobes of the brain, which are believed to play an important role in memory for events.
Episodic memory	Episodic memory is the explicit memory of events. It includes time, place, and associated emotions (which affect the quality of the memorization).
Semantic memory	Semantic memory refers to the memory of meanings, understandings, and other knowledge.
Baddeley	Baddeley introduced a multicomponent model of working memory for the temporary maintenance and manipulation of information. It emphasizes the functional importance of such a system rather than its use as the unitary short-term store proposed by Atkinson and Shiffrin.
Hippocampus	The hippocampus is a part of the brain located inside the temporal lobe. It forms a part of the limbic system and plays a part in memory and navigation.
Lesion	A lesion is a non-specific term referring to abnormal tissue in the body. It can be caused by any disease process including trauma (physical, chemical, electrical), infection, neoplasm, metabolic and autoimmune.
Evolution	Commonly used to refer to gradual change, evolution is the change in the frequency of alleles within a population from one generation to the next. This change may be caused by different mechanisms, including natural selection, genetic drift, or changes in population (gene flow).
Ischemia	Narrowing of arteries caused by plaque buildup within the arteries is called ischemia.
Gyrus	A gyrus is a ridge on the cerebral cortex. It is generally surrounded by one or more sulci.
Syndrome	The term syndrome is the association of several clinically recognizable features, signs, symptoms, phenomena or characteristics which often occur together, so that the presence of one feature indicates the presence of the others.
Personality	Personality refers to the pattern of enduring characteristics that differentiates a person,

	the patterns of behaviors that make each individual unique.
Stages	Stages represent relatively discrete periods of time in which functioning is qualitatively different from functioning at other periods.
Liver	The liver plays a major role in metabolism and has a number of functions in the body including detoxification, glycogen storage and plasma protein synthesis. It also produces bile, which is important for digestion. The liver converts most carbohydrates, proteing, and fats into glucose.
Cerebellum	The cerebellum is located in the inferior posterior portion of the head (the hindbrain), directly dorsal to the brainstem and pons, inferior to the occipital lobe. The cerebellum is a region of the brain that plays an important role in the integration of sensory perception and fine motor output.
Hypothalamus	The hypothalamus is a region of the brain located below the thalamus, forming the major portion of the ventral region of the diencephalon and functioning to regulate certain metabolic processes and other autonomic activities.
Diencephalon	The diencephalon is the region of the brain that includes the epithalamus, thalamus, and hypothalamus. It is located above the mesencephalon of the brain stem. Sensory information is relayed between the brain stem and the rest of the brain regions
Sullivan	Sullivan developed the Self System, a configuration of the personality traits developed in childhood and reinforced by positive affirmation and the security operations developed in childhood to avoid anxiety and threats to self-esteem.
Thalamus	An area near the center of the brain involved in the relay of sensory information to the cortex and in the functions of sleep and attention is the thalamus.
Insidious onset	An insidious onset refers to the development of a disorder gradually over an extended period of time.
Retrograde amnesia	Retrograde amnesia is a form of amnesia where someone will be unable to recall events that occurred before the onset of amnesia.
Stroke	A stroke occurs when the blood supply to a part of the brain is suddenly interrupted by occlusion, by hemorrhage, or other causes
Forebrain	The forebrain is the highest level of the brain. Key structures in the forebrain are the limbic system, thalamus, basal ganglia, hypothalamus, and cerebral cortex.
Mammillary body	The mammillary body is a pair of small round bodies in the brain forming part of the limbic system. Symptoms from damage to the mammillary bodies can include impaired memory, also called anterograde amnesia; this suggests that the mammillary bodies might be important for memory.
Acetylcholine	The chemical compound acetylcholine was the first neurotransmitter to be identified. It plays a role in learning, memory, and rapid eye movement sleep and causes the skeletal muscle fibers to contract.
Dementia	Dementia is progressive decline in cognitive function due to damage or disease in the brain beyond what might be expected from normal aging.
Prefrontal cortex	The prefrontal cortex is the anterior part of the frontal lobes of the brain, lying in front of the motor and associative areas. It has been implicated in planning complex cognitive behaviors, personality expression and moderating correct social behavior. The prefrontal cortex continues to develop until around age 6.
Concussion	Concussion, or mild traumatic brain injury (MTBI), is the most common and least serious type of brain injury. A milder type of diffuse axonal injury, concussion involves a transient loss

	of mental function. It can be caused by acceleration or deceleration forces, by a direct blow, or by penetrating injuries.
Hebb	Hebb demonstrated that the rearing of rats in an enriched environment could alter neural development and that sensory - neural connections were shaped by experience. He is famous for developing the concept of neural nets. He also believed that learning early in life is of the incremental variety, whereas later it is cognitive, insightful, and more all-or-none.
Memory consolidation	The broad definition of memory consolidation is the process by which recent memories are crystallized into long-term memory.
Electroconvu-sive shock	Electroconvulsive shock is a type of psychiatric shock therapy involving the induction of an artificial seizure in a patient by passing electricity through the brain.
Electrode	Any device used to electrically stimulate nerve tissue or to record its activity is an electrode.
Depression	In everyday language depression refers to any downturn in mood, which may be relatively transitory and perhaps due to something trivial. This is differentiated from Clinical depression which is marked by symptoms that last two weeks or more and are so severe that they interfere with daily living.
Consciousness	The awareness of the sensations, thoughts, and feelings being experienced at a given moment is called consciousness.
Habituation	In habituation there is a progressive reduction in the response probability with continued repetition of a stimulus.
Control group	A group that does not receive the treatment effect in an experiment is referred to as the control group or sometimes as the comparison group.
Construct	A generalized concept, such as anxiety or gravity, is a construct.
Labile	Easily emotionally moved, quickly shifting from one emotion to another, or easily aroused is referred to as labile.
Theories	Theories are logically self-consistent models or frameworks describing the behavior of a certain natural or social phenomenon. They are broad explanations and predictions concerning phenomena of interest.
Engram	An engram is said to be a memory trace, one possible explanation for the persistence of memory. Fundamentally, an engram is posited to be a physical, biochemical change in the brain (and other neural tissue) in response to external stimuli, thus forming a memory.
Species	Species refers to a reproductively isolated breeding population.
Neuroanatomy	Neuroanatomy is the study of the anatomy of the central nervous system.
Amygdala	Located in the brain's medial temporal lobe, the almond-shaped amygdala is believed to play a key role in the emotions. It forms part of the limbic system and is linked to both fear responses and pleasure. Its size is positively correlated with aggressive behavior across species.
Validity	The extent to which a test measures what it is intended to measure is called validity.
Pinel	Pinel is regarded as the father of modern psychiatry. He was a clinician believing that medical truth derived from clinical experience. While at Bicêtre, Pinel did away with bleeding, purging, and blistering in favor a therapy that involved close contact with and careful observation of patients.
Neocortex	The neocortex is part of the cerebral cortex which covers most of the surface of the cerebral hemispheres including the frontal, parietal, occipital, and temporal lobes. Often seen as the

	hallmark of human intelligence, the role of this structure in the brain appears to be involved in conscious thought, spatial reasoning, and sensory perception.
Resurgence	Resurgence refers to the reappearance during extinction, of a previously reinforced behavior.
Hypothesis	A specific statement about behavior or mental processes that is testable through research is a hypothesis.
Working Memory	Working memory is the collection of structures and processes in the brain used for temporarily storing and manipulating information. Working memory consists of both memory for items that are currently being processed, and components governing attention and directing the processing itself.
Neuron	The neuron is the primary cell of the nervous system. They are found in the brain, the spinal cord, in the nerves and ganglia of the peripheral nervous system. It is a specialized cell that conducts impulses through the nervous system and contains three major parts: cell body, dendrites, and an axon. It can have many dendrites but only one axon.
Premise	A premise is a statement presumed true within the context of a discourse, especially of a logical argument.
Nucleus	In neuroanatomy, a cluster of cell bodies of neurons within the central nervous system is a nucleus.
Sensory memory	Sensory memory is our ability to retain impressions of sensory information after the original stimulus has ceased.
Retrieval	Retrieval is the location of stored information and its subsequent return to consciousness. It is the third stage of information processing.
Stimulus	A change in an environmental condition that elicits a response is a stimulus.
Neutral stimulus	A stimulus prior to conditioning that does not naturally result in the response of interest is called a neutral stimulus.
Penfield	Penfield treated patients with severe epilepsy by destroying nerve cells in the brain. Before operating, he stimulated the brain with electrical probes while the patients were conscious on the operating table, and observed their responses. It allowed him to create maps of sensory and motor functions.
Perception	Perception is the process of acquiring, interpreting, selecting, and organizing sensory information.
Paradigm	Paradigm refers to the set of practices that defines a scientific discipline during a particular period of time. It provides a framework from which to conduct research, it ensures that a certain range of phenomena, those on which the paradigm focuses, are explored thoroughly. Itmay also blind scientists to other, perhaps more fruitful, ways of dealing with their subject matter.
Conditional stimulus	A conditional stimulus in a conditional reflex elicits a conditional response.
Habit	A habit is a response that has become completely separated from its eliciting stimulus. Early learning theorists used the term to describe S-R associations, however not all S-R associations become a habit, rather many are extinguished after reinforcement is withdrawn.
Synapse	A synapse is specialized junction through which cells of the nervous system signal to one another and to non-neuronal cells such as muscles or glands.
Baseline	Measure of a particular behavior or process taken before the introduction of the independent variable or treatment is called the baseline.

Population	Population refers to all members of a well-defined group of organisms, events, or things.
Amplitude	Amplitude is a nonnegative scalar measure of a wave's magnitude of oscillation.
Nervous system	The body's electrochemical communication circuitry, made up of billions of neurons is a nervous system.
Glutamate	Glutamate is one of the 20 standard amino acids used by all organisms in their proteins. It is critical for proper cell function, but it is not an essential nutrient in humans because it can be manufactured from other compounds.
Receptor	A sensory receptor is a structure that recognizes a stimulus in the internal or external environment of an organism. In response to stimuli the sensory receptor initiates sensory transduction by creating graded potentials or action potentials in the same cell or in an adjacent one.
Neurotransmitter	A neurotransmitter is a chemical that is used to relay, amplify and modulate electrical signals between a neurons and another cell.
Neural network	A clusters of neurons that is interconnected to process information is referred to as a neural network.
Ion	An ion is an atom or group of atoms with a net electric charge. The energy required to detach an electron in its lowest energy state from an atom or molecule of a gas with less net electric charge is called the ionization potential, or ionization energy.
Axon terminal	A swelling at the end of an axon that is designed to release a chemical substance onto another neuron, muscle cell, or gland cell is called the axon terminal.
Axon	An axon, or "nerve fiber," is a long slender projection of a nerve cell, or "neuron," which conducts electrical impulses away from the neuron's cell body or soma.
Cytoplasm	Cytoplasm is the colloidal, semi-fluid matter contained within the cell's plasma membrane, in which organelles are suspended. In contrast to the protoplasm, the cytoplasm does not include the cell nucleus, the interior of which is made up of nucleoplasm.
Protein	A protein is a complex, high-molecular-weight organic compound that consists of amino acids joined by peptide bonds. It is essential to the structure and function of all living cells and viruses. Many are enzymes or subunits of enzymes.
Enzyme	An enzyme is a protein that catalyzes, or speeds up, a chemical reaction. Enzymes are essential to sustain life because most chemical reactions in biological cells would occur too slowly, or would lead to different products, without enzymes.
Dendritic spine	A dendritic spine is a small membranous extrusion that protrudes from a dendrite and forms one half of a synapse. Changes in dendritic spine density underlie many brain functions, including motivation, learning, and memory. In particular, long-term memory is mediated in part by the growth of new dendritic spines to reinforce a particular neural pathway.
Variability	Statistically, variability refers to how much the scores in a distribution spread out, away from the mean.
Terminal buttons	Terminal buttons are small bulges at the end of axons that send messages to other neurons.
Plasticity	The capacity for modification and change is referred to as plasticity.
Dissociation	Dissociation is a psychological state or condition in which certain thoughts, emotions, sensations, or memories are separated from the rest.
Affect	A subjective feeling or emotional tone often accompanied by bodily expressions noticeable to others is called affect.

Case study	A carefully drawn biography that may be obtained through interviews, questionnaires, and psychological tests is called a case study.
Anatomy	Anatomy is the branch of biology that deals with the structure and organization of living things. It can be divided into animal anatomy (zootomy) and plant anatomy (phytonomy). Major branches of anatomy include comparative anatomy, histology, and human anatomy.

Population	Population refers to all members of a well-defined group of organisms, events, or things.
Obesity	The state of being more than 20 percent above the average weight for a person of one's height is called obesity.
Anorexia	Anorexia nervosa is an eating disorder characterized by voluntary starvation and exercise stress.
Set point	Set point refers to any one of a number of quantities (e.g. body weight, body temperature) which the body tries to keep at a particular value
Eating disorders	Psychological disorders characterized by distortion of the body image and gross disturbances in eating patterns are called eating disorders.
Temporal lobe	The temporal lobe is part of the cerebrum. It lies at the side of the brain, beneath the lateral or Sylvian fissure. Adjacent areas in the superior, posterior and lateral parts of the temporal lobe are involved in high-level auditory processing.
Amnesia	Amnesia is a condition in which memory is disturbed. The causes of amnesia are organic or functional. Organic causes include damage to the brain, through trauma or disease, or use of certain (generally sedative) drugs.
Lobes	The four major sections of the cerebral cortex: frontal, parietal, temporal, and occipital are called lobes.
Motivation	In psychology, motivation is the driving force (desire) behind all actions of an organism.
Amino acid	Amino acid is the basic structural building unit of proteins. They form short polymer chains called peptides or polypeptides which in turn form structures called proteins.
Protein	A protein is a complex, high-molecular-weight organic compound that consists of amino acids joined by peptide bonds. It is essential to the structure and function of all living cells and viruses. Many are enzymes or subunits of enzymes.
Enzyme	An enzyme is a protein that catalyzes, or speeds up, a chemical reaction. Enzymes are essential to sustain life because most chemical reactions in biological cells would occur too slowly, or would lead to different products, without enzymes.
Gall	Gall most noted for introducing phrenology, was correct in assigning the brain the role of the seat of mental activities, and although he was wrong in detail due to a faulty methodology, the possibility of the localization of brain functions is widely accepted today.
Liver	The liver plays a major role in metabolism and has a number of functions in the body including detoxification, glycogen storage and plasma protein synthesis. It also produces bile, which is important for digestion. The liver converts most carbohydrates, proteing, and fats into glucose.
Glucose	Glucose, a simple monosaccharide sugar, is one of the most important carbohydrates and is used as a source of energy in animals and plants. Glucose is one of the main products of photosynthesis and starts respiration.
Metabolism	Metabolism is the biochemical modification of chemical compounds in living organisms and cells.
Hormone	A hormone is a chemical messenger from one cell (or group of cells) to another. The best known are those produced by endocrine glands, but they are produced by nearly every organ system. The function of hormones is to serve as a signal to the target cells; the action of the hormone is determined by the pattern of secretion and the signal transduction of the receiving tissue.
Pancreas	The pancreas is a retroperitoneal organ that serves two functions: it produces juice

	containing digestive enzymes; and it produces several important hormones including insulin, glucagon, and several other hormones.
Brain	The brain controls and coordinates most movement, behavior and homeostatic body functions such as heartbeat, blood pressure, fluid balance and body temperature. Functions of the brain are responsible for cognition, emotion, memory, motor learning and other sorts of learning. The brain is primarily made up of two types of cells: glia and neurons.
Pinel	Pinel is regarded as the father of modern psychiatry. He was a clinician believing that medical truth derived from clinical experience. While at Bicêtre, Pinel did away with bleeding, purging, and blistering in favor a therapy that involved close contact with and careful observation of patients.
Theories	Theories are logically self-consistent models or frameworks describing the behavior of a certain natural or social phenomenon. They are broad explanations and predictions concerning phenomena of interest.
Feedback	Feedback refers to information returned to a person about the effects a response has had.
Negative feedback	In negative feedback, the output of a system is added back into the input, so as to reverse the direction of change. This tends to keep the output from changing, so it is stabilizing and attempts to maintain homeostasis.
Homeostasis	Homeostasis is the property of an open system, especially living organisms, to regulate its internal environment so as to maintain a stable condition, by means of multiple dynamic equilibrium adjustments controlled by interrelated regulation mechanisms.
Bolles	Bolles proposes that a response can be rapidly acquired only if it is a Species Specific Defense Response. He also argues that a response can be acquired only by the suppression of other SSDR's. Learning is the formation of expectancies, classical conditioning is the formation of S-S expectancies, operant conditioning is the development of R-S expectancies.
Attachment	Attachment is the tendency to seek closeness to another person and feel secure when that person is present.
Society	The social sciences use the term society to mean a group of people that form a semi-closed (or semi-open) social system, in which most interactions are with other individuals belonging to the group.
Species	Species refers to a reproductively isolated breeding population.
Norms	In testing, standards of test performance that permit the comparison of one person's score on the test to the scores of others who have taken the same test are referred to as norms.
Sensation	Sensation is the first stage in the chain of biochemical and neurologic events that begins with the impinging of a stimulus upon the receptor cells of a sensory organ, which then leads to perception, the mental state that is reflected in statements like "I see a uniformly blue wall."
Conditioning	Conditioning describes the process by which behaviors can be learned or modified through interaction with the environment.
Pavlovian conditioning	Pavlovian conditioning, synonymous with classical conditioning is a type of learning found in animals, caused by the association (or pairing) of two stimuli or what Ivan Pavlov described as the learning of conditional behavior, therefore called conditioning.
Stimulus	A change in an environmental condition that elicits a response is a stimulus.
Conditional stimulus	A conditional stimulus in a conditional reflex elicits a conditional response.

Satiety	Satiety refers to the state of being satisfied; fullness.
Motivational state	A motivational state is an internal, reversible condition in an individual that orients the individual toward one or another type of goal. This condition is not observed directly but is inferred from the individual's behavior.
Baseline	Measure of a particular behavior or process taken before the introduction of the independent variable or treatment is called the baseline.
Social influence	Social influence is when the actions or thoughts of individual(s) are changed by other individual(s). Peer pressure is an example of social influence.
Malnutrition	Malnutrition is a general term for the medical condition in a person or animal caused by an unbalanced diet—either too little or too much food, or a diet missing one or more important nutrients.
Satiety center	Satiety, or the feeling of fullness and disappearance of appetite after a meal, is a process mediated by the ventromedial nucleus in the hypothalamus. It is therefore the satiety center.
Hypothalamus	The hypothalamus is a region of the brain located below the thalamus, forming the major portion of the ventral region of the diencephalon and functioning to regulate certain metabolic processes and other autonomic activities.
Syndrome	The term syndrome is the association of several clinically recognizable features, signs, symptoms, phenomena or characteristics which often occur together, so that the presence of one feature indicates the presence of the others.
Lesion	A lesion is a non-specific term referring to abnormal tissue in the body. It can be caused by any disease process including trauma (physical, chemical, electrical), infection, neoplasm, metabolic and autoimmune.
Ventromedial hypothalamus	Ventromedial hypothalamus acts as a satiety center and, when activated, signals an animal to stop eating; when destroyed, the animal overeats, becoming obese.
Consciousness	The awareness of the sensations, thoughts, and feelings being experienced at a given moment is called consciousness.
Deprivation	Deprivation, is the loss or withholding of normal stimulation, nutrition, comfort, love, and so forth; a condition of lacking. The level of stimulation is less than what is required.
Aphagia	Aphagia is an inpairment in the ability to eat.
Hyperphagic	Hyperphagic is the term for extreme over-eating.
Aphagic	Aphagic is the term for extreme under-eating.
Nucleus	In neuroanatomy, a cluster of cell bodies of neurons within the central nervous system is a nucleus.
Gastrointestinal tract	The gastrointestinal tract is the system of organs within multicellular animals which takes in food, digests it to extract energy and nutrients, and expels the remaining waste.
Resurgence	Resurgence refers to the reappearance during extinction, of a previously reinforced behavior.
Nerve	A nerve is an enclosed, cable-like bundle of nerve fibers or axons, which includes the glia that ensheath the axons in myelin. Neurons are sometimes called nerve cells, though this term is technically imprecise since many neurons do not form nerves.
Peptides	Peptides are the family of molecules formed from the linking, in a defined order, of various amino acids.
Neurotransmitter	A neurotransmitter is a chemical that is used to relay, amplify and modulate electrical signals between a neurons and another cell.

Receptor | A sensory receptor is a structure that recognizes a stimulus in the internal or external environment of an organism. In response to stimuli the sensory receptor initiates sensory transduction by creating graded potentials or action potentials in the same cell or in an adjacent one.

Hypothesis | A specific statement about behavior or mental processes that is testable through research is a hypothesis.

Beck | Beck was initially trained as a psychoanalyst and conducted research on the psychoanalytic treatment of depression. With out the strong ability to collect data to this end, he began exploring cognitive approaches to treatment and originated cognitive behavior therapy.

Conditioned taste aversion | A procedure in which an animal drinks a flavored solution and is then made sick by a toxin is conditioned taste aversion, called the Garcia Effect. Both the long time interval between CS and CR and that only a single trial is necessary for the conditioning challenges normal conditioning tenets.

Neuropeptide Y | Neuropeptide Y is a 36 amino acid peptide neurotransmitter found in the brain and autonomic nervous system. It has been associated with a number of physiologic processes in the brain, including the regulation of energy balance, memory and learning, and epilepsy.

Ghrelin | Ghrelin is a hormone that is produced by cells lining the stomach and stimulates the appetite. Ghrelin levels are increased prior to a meal and decreased after a meal. It is considered the counterpart of the hormone leptin, produced by adipose tissue, which induces satiation when present at higher levels.

Orexin | Orexin is the common name given to a pair of highly excititory neuropeptide hormones that were simultaneously discovered by two groups of reseachers in rat brains. The University of Texas, coined the term orexin to reflect the appetite-stimulating activity of these hormones.

Serotonin | Serotonin, a neurotransmitter, is believed to play an important part of the biochemistry of depression, bipolar disorder and anxiety. It is also believed to be influential on sexuality and appetite.

Agonist | Agonist refers to a drug that mimics or increases a neurotransmitter's effects.

Variability | Statistically, variability refers to how much the scores in a distribution spread out, away from the mean.

Immune response | The body's defensive reaction to invasion by bacteria, viral agents, or other foreign substances is called the immune response.

Life span | Life span refers to the upper boundary of life, the maximum number of years an individual can live. The maximum life span of human beings is about 120 years of age. Females live an average of 6 years longer than males.

Correlation | A statistical technique for determining the degree of association between two or more variables is referred to as correlation.

Premise | A premise is a statement presumed true within the context of a discourse, especially of a logical argument.

Metabolic rate | Metabolic rate refers to the rate at which the body burns calories to produce energy.

Basal metabolic rate | Basal metabolic rate is the rate of metabolism when an individual is at rest in a warm environment and is in the post absorptive state, and has not eaten for at least 12 hours.

Neuron | The neuron is the primary cell of the nervous system. They are found in the brain, the spinal cord, in the nerves and ganglia of the peripheral nervous system. It is a specialized cell that conducts impulses through the nervous system and contains three major parts: cell body, dendrites, and an axon. It can have many dendrites but only one axon.

Resting potential	The resting potential of a cell is the membrane potential that would be maintained if there were no action potentials, synaptic potentials, or other active changes in the membrane potential. In most cells the resting potential has a negative value, which by convention means that there is excess negative charge inside compared to outside.
Analogy	An analogy is a comparison between two different things, in order to highlight some form of similarity. Analogy is the cognitive process of transferring information from a particular subject to another particular subject.
Affect	A subjective feeling or emotional tone often accompanied by bodily expressions noticeable to others is called affect.
Biopsychologist	A psychologist who studies the relationship between behavior and biological processes, especially activity in the nervous system is referred to as a Biopsychologist.
Insight	Insight refers to a sudden awareness of the relationships among various elements that had previously appeared to be independent of one another.
Individual differences	Individual differences psychology studies the ways in which individual people differ in their behavior. This is distinguished from other aspects of psychology in that although psychology is ostensibly a study of individuals, modern psychologists invariably study groups.
Evolution	Commonly used to refer to gradual change, evolution is the change in the frequency of alleles within a population from one generation to the next. This change may be caused by different mechanisms, including natural selection, genetic drift, or changes in population (gene flow).
Incentive value	The value of a goal above and beyond its ability to fill a need is its incentive value.
Incentive	An incentive is what is expected once a behavior is performed. An incentive acts as a reinforcer.
Stages	Stages represent relatively discrete periods of time in which functioning is qualitatively different from functioning at other periods.
Mutation	Mutation is a permanent, sometimes transmissible (if the change is to a germ cell) change to the genetic material (usually DNA or RNA) of a cell. They can be caused by copying errors in the genetic material during cell division and by exposure to radiation, chemicals, or viruses, or can occur deliberately under cellular control during the processes such as meiosis or hypermutation.
Leptin	Leptin refers to a hormone produced by fat cells that acts in the brain to inhibit hunger and regulate body weight.
Fat cells	Fat cells serve as storehouses for liquefied fat in the body and that number from 25 to 35 billion in normal weight individuals; with weight loss, they decrease in size but not in number.
Gene	A gene is an ultramicroscopic area of the chromosome. It is the smallest physical unit of the DNA molecule that carries a piece of hereditary information.
Binge	Binge refers to relatively brief episode of uncontrolled, excessive consumption.
Bulimia	Bulimia refers to a disorder in which a person binges on incredibly large quantities of food, then purges by vomiting or by using laxatives. Bulimia is often less about food, and more to do with deep psychological issues and profound feelings of lack of control.
Etiology	Etiology is the study of causation. The term is used in philosophy, physics and biology in reference to the causes of various phenomena. It is generally the study of why things occur, or even the reasons behind the way that things act.
Learning	Learning is a relatively permanent change in behavior that results from experience. Thus, to

attribute a behavioral change to learning, the change must be relatively permanent and must result from experience.

Gland	A gland is an organ in an animal's body that synthesizes a substance for release such as hormones, often into the bloodstream or into cavities inside the body or its outer surface.
Hormone	A hormone is a chemical messenger from one cell (or group of cells) to another. The best known are those produced by endocrine glands, but they are produced by nearly every organ system. The function of hormones is to serve as a signal to the target cells; the action of the hormone is determined by the pattern of secretion and the signal transduction of the receiving tissue.
Attitude	An enduring mental representation of a person, place, or thing that evokes an emotional response and related behavior is called attitude.
Endocrine gland	An endocrine gland is one of a set of internal organs involved in the secretion of hormones into the blood. The other major type of gland is the exocrine glands, which secrete substances—usually digestive juices—into the digestive tract or onto the skin.
Nervous system	The body's electrochemical communication circuitry, made up of billions of neurons is a nervous system.
Amino acid	Amino acid is the basic structural building unit of proteins. They form short polymer chains called peptides or polypeptides which in turn form structures called proteins.
Peptides	Peptides are the family of molecules formed from the linking, in a defined order, of various amino acids.
Steroid	A steroid is a lipid characterized by a carbon skeleton with four fused rings. Different steroids vary in the functional groups attached to these rings. Hundreds of distinct steroids have been identified in plants and animals. Their most important role in most living systems is as hormones.
Protein	A protein is a complex, high-molecular-weight organic compound that consists of amino acids joined by peptide bonds. It is essential to the structure and function of all living cells and viruses. Many are enzymes or subunits of enzymes.
Epinephrine	Epinephrine is a hormone and a neurotransmitter. Epinephrine plays a central role in the short-term stress reaction—the physiological response to threatening or exciting conditions. It is secreted by the adrenal medulla. When released into the bloodstream, epinephrine binds to multiple receptors and has numerous effects throughout the body.
Tyrosine	Tyrosine is one of the 20 amino acids that are used by cells to synthesize proteins. It plays a key role in signal transduction, since it can be tagged (phosphorylated) with a phosphate group by protein kinases to alter the functionality and activity of certain enzymes.
Adrenal medulla	Composed mainly of hormone-producing chromaffin cells, the adrenal medulla is the principal site of the conversion of the amino acid tyrosine into the catecholamines epinephrine and norepinephrine (also called adrenaline and noradrenaline, respectively).
Cholesterol	Cholesterol is a steroid, a lipid, and an alcohol, found in the cell membranes of all body tissues, and transported in the blood plasma of all animals. Cholesterol is an important component of the membranes of cells, providing stability; it makes the membrane's fluidity stable over a bigger temperature interval.
Cell membrane	A component of every biological cell, the selectively permeable cell membrane is a thin and structured bilayer of phospholipid and protein molecules that envelopes the cell. It separates a cell's interior from its surroundings and controls what moves in and out.
Receptor	A sensory receptor is a structure that recognizes a stimulus in the internal or external environment of an organism. In response to stimuli the sensory receptor initiates sensory transduction by creating graded potentials or action potentials in the same cell or in an adjacent one.

Affect | A subjective feeling or emotional tone often accompanied by bodily expressions noticeable to others is called affect.

Cytoplasm | Cytoplasm is the colloidal, semi-fluid matter contained within the cell's plasma membrane, in which organelles are suspended. In contrast to the protoplasm, the cytoplasm does not include the cell nucleus, the interior of which is made up of nucleoplasm.

Nucleus | In neuroanatomy, a cluster of cell bodies of neurons within the central nervous system is a nucleus.

Gene | A gene is an ultramicroscopic area of the chromosome. It is the smallest physical unit of the DNA molecule that carries a piece of hereditary information.

Gonads | The gonads are the organs that make gametes. Gametes are haploid germ cells. For example, sperm and egg cells are gametes. In the male the gonads are the testicles, and in the female the gonads are the ovaries.

Testes | Testes are the male reproductive glands or gonads; this is where sperm develop and are stored.

Ovary | The female reproductive organ is the ovary. It performs two major functions: producing eggs and secreting hormones.

Zygote | A zygote is a cell that is the result of fertilization. That is, two haploid cells—usually (but not always) a sperm cell from a male and an ovum from a female—merge into a single diploid cell called the zygote.

Ovum | Ovum is a female sex cell or gamete.

Chromosome | The DNA which carries genetic information in biological cells is normally packaged in the form of one or more large macromolecules called a chromosome. Humans normally have 46.

Sex chromosomes | The sex chromosomes are the 23rd pair of chromosomes. They determine whether the child will be male or female. A pair with two X-shaped chromosomes produces a female. A pair with an X chromosome and a Y chromosome produces a male.

X chromosome | The sex chromosomes are one of the 23 pairs of human chromosomes. Each person normally has one pair of sex chromosomes in each cell. Females have two X chromosomes, while males have one X and one Y chromosome. The X chromosome carries hundreds of genes but few, if any, of these have anything to do directly with sex determination.

Y chromosome | The Y chromosome is one of the two sex chromosomes in humans and most other mammals. The sex chromosomes are one of the 23 pairs of human chromosomes. The Y chromosome contains the fewest genes of any of the chromosomes. It contains the genes that cause testis development, thus determining maleness. It is usually contributed by the father.

Testosterone | Testosterone is a steroid hormone from the androgen group. It is the principal male sex hormone and the "original" anabolic steroid.

Estradiol | Estradiol is a sex hormone. Labelled the "female" hormone but also present in males it represents the major estrogen in humans. Critical for sexual functioning estradiol also supports bone growth.

Estrogen | Estrogen is a group of steroid compounds that function as the primary female sex hormone. They are produced primarily by developing follicles in the ovaries, the corpus luteum and the placenta.

Androgen | Androgen is the generic term for any natural or synthetic compound, usually a steroid hormone, that stimulates or controls the development and maintenance of masculine characteristics in vertebrates by binding to androgen receptors.

Progestin	A hormone used to maintain pregnancy that can cause masculinization of the fetus is progestin.
Progesterone	A female sex hormone that promotes growth of the sex organs and helps maintain pregnancy is called progesterone.
Uterus	The uterus or womb is the major female reproductive organ. The main function of the uterus is to accept a fertilized ovum which becomes implanted into the endometrium, and derives nourishment from blood vessels which develop exclusively for this purpose.
Adrenal cortex	Adrenal cortex refers to the outer layer of the adrenal glands, which produces hormones that affect salt intake, reactions to stress, and sexual development.
Adrenal glands	The adrenal glands sit atop the kidneys. They are chiefly responsible for regulating the stress response through the synthesis of corticosteroids and catecholamines, including cortisol and adrenalin.
Glucose	Glucose, a simple monosaccharide sugar, is one of the most important carbohydrates and is used as a source of energy in animals and plants. Glucose is one of the main products of photosynthesis and starts respiration.
Pituitary gland	The pituitary gland is an endocrine gland about the size of a pea that sits in the small, bony cavity at the base of the brain. The pituitary gland secretes hormones regulating a wide variety of bodily activities, including trophic hormones that stimulate other endocrine glands.
Optic chiasm	Optic chiasm refers to the point at which the optic nerves from the inside half of each eye cross over and then project to the opposite half of the brain.
Hypothalamus	The hypothalamus is a region of the brain located below the thalamus, forming the major portion of the ventral region of the diencephalon and functioning to regulate certain metabolic processes and other autonomic activities.
Lesion	A lesion is a non-specific term referring to abnormal tissue in the body. It can be caused by any disease process including trauma (physical, chemical, electrical), infection, neoplasm, metabolic and autoimmune.
Oxytocin	Oxytocin is synthesized in magnocellular neurosecretory cells in the hypothalamus and released by the posterior lobe of the pituitary gland. It is involved in the facilitation of birth and breastfeeding as well as in bonding.
Neuron	The neuron is the primary cell of the nervous system. They are found in the brain, the spinal cord, in the nerves and ganglia of the peripheral nervous system. It is a specialized cell that conducts impulses through the nervous system and contains three major parts: cell body, dendrites, and an axon. It can have many dendrites but only one axon.
Axon	An axon, or "nerve fiber," is a long slender projection of a nerve cell, or "neuron," which conducts electrical impulses away from the neuron's cell body or soma.
Action potential	The electrical impulse that provides the basis for the conduction of a neural impulse along an axon of a neuron is the action potential. When a biological cell or patch of membrane undergoes an action potential, or electrical excitation, the polarity of the transmembrane voltage swings rapidly from negative to positive and back.
Antidiuretic hormone	Antidiuretic hormone is a peptide hormone produced by the hypothalamus, and stored in the posterior part of the pituitary gland. It acts on the kidneys, concentrating the urine by promoting the reabsorption of water from the cortical collecting duct.
Hypothesis	A specific statement about behavior or mental processes that is testable through research is a hypothesis.

Terminal buttons	Terminal buttons are small bulges at the end of axons that send messages to other neurons.
Capillary	The capillary is the smallest of a body's blood vessels, measuring 5-10 ìm. They connect arteries and veins, and most closely interact with tissues.
Thyroid Gland	The thyroid gland is an endocrine gland. It is situated on the front side of the neck just below the Adam's apple. The primary function of the thyroid is production of hormones such as thyroxine.
Thyroid	In anatomy, the thyroid is the largest endocrine gland in the body. The primary function of the thyroid is production of hormones.
Gonadotropins	Gonadotropins are protein hormones secreted by the pituitary gland. The gonads -- testes and ovaries -- are the primary target organs. The gonadotropins stimulates the testes and the ovaries to produce testosterone (and indirectly estradiol).
Luteinizing hormone	Luteinizing hormone is a hormone synthesised and secreted by gonadotropes in the anterior lobe of the pituitary gland. It is one of the gonadotropins, which are necessary for proper sexual function, the other being follicle stimulating hormone
Parasympathetic	The parasympathetic nervous system is one of two divisions of the autonomic nervous system. It conserves energy as it slows the heart rate, increases intestinal and gland activity, and relaxes sphincter muscles. In another words, it acts to reverse the effects of the Sympathetic nervous system.
Sympathetic	The sympathetic nervous system activates what is often termed the "fight or flight response". It is an automatic regulation system, that is, one that operates without the intervention of conscious thought.
Brain	The brain controls and coordinates most movement, behavior and homeostatic body functions such as heartbeat, blood pressure, fluid balance and body temperature. Functions of the brain are responsible for cognition, emotion, memory, motor learning and other sorts of learning. The brain is primarily made up of two types of cells: glia and neurons.
Autonomic nervous system	A division of the peripheral nervous system, the autonomic nervous system, regulates glands and activities such as heartbeat, respiration, digestion, and dilation of the pupils. It is responsible for homeostasis, maintaining a relatively constant internal environment .
Feedback	Feedback refers to information returned to a person about the effects a response has had.
Negative feedback	In negative feedback, the output of a system is added back into the input, so as to reverse the direction of change. This tends to keep the output from changing, so it is stabilizing and attempts to maintain homeostasis.
Fetus	A fetus develops from the end of the 8th week of pregnancy (when the major structures have formed), until birth.
Antigen	An antigen is a molecule that stimulates the production of antibodies. Usually, it is a protein or a polysaccharide, but can be any type of molecule, including small molecules (haptens) coupled to a protein (carrier).
Fallopian tube	A tube through which the eggs travel from the ovaries to the uterus is a fallopian tube.
Vas deferens	The vas deferens are two muscular tubes that carry sperm from the testes to the urethra.
Seminal vesicles	The seminal vesicles are a pair of glands on the posterior surface of the urinary bladder of males. They secrete a significant proportion of the fluid that ultimately becomes semen.
Scrotum	The scrotum is an external sack of skin that holds the testes.
Fetal period	The prenatal period of development that begins 2 months after conception and lasts for 7 months, on the average is called the fetal period.

Antecedents	In behavior modification, events that typically precede the target response are called antecedents.
Genitals	Genitals refers to the internal and external reproductive organs.
Clitoris	Clitoris refers to an external female sex organ that is highly sensitive to sexual stimulation.
Labia	The major and minor lips of the female genitalia are called labia.
Penis	The penis is the external male copulatory organ and the external male organ of urination. In humans, the penis is homologous to the female clitoris, as it develops from the same embryonic structure. It is capable of erection for use in copulation.
Synapse	A synapse is specialized junction through which cells of the nervous system signal to one another and to non-neuronal cells such as muscles or glands.
Glial	Glial cells are non-neuronal cells that provide support and nutrition, maintain homeostasis, form myelin, and participate in signal transmission in the nervous system.
Perinatal	Perinatal is the period occurring around the time of birth (5 months before and 1 month after).
Species	Species refers to a reproductively isolated breeding population.
Stages	Stages represent relatively discrete periods of time in which functioning is qualitatively different from functioning at other periods.
Ejaculation	Ejaculation is the process of ejecting semen from the penis, and is usually accompanied by orgasm as a result of sexual stimulation.
Adler	Adler argued that human personality could be explained teleologically, separate strands dominated by the guiding purpose of the individual's unconscious self ideal to convert feelings of inferiority to superiority (or rather completeness). The desires of the self ideal were countered by social and ethical demands.
Secondary sex characteristics	Secondary sex characteristics are traits that distinguish the two sexes of a species, but that are not directly part of the reproductive system.
Secondary sex characteristic	A secondary sex characteristic is a trait that distinguishes the two sexes of a species, but is not directly part of the reproductive system.
Puberty	Puberty refers to the process of physical changes by which a child's body becomes an adult body capable of reproduction.
Growth hormone	Growth hormone is a polypeptide hormone synthesised and secreted by the anterior pituitary gland which stimulates growth and cell reproduction in humans and other vertebrate animals.
Maturation	The orderly unfolding of traits, as regulated by the genetic code is called maturation.
Larynx	The larynx, or voicebox, is an organ in the neck of mammals involved in protection of the trachea and sound production. The larynx houses the vocal cords, and is situated at the point where the upper tract splits into the trachea and the esophagus.
Socioeconomic	Socioeconomic pertains to the study of the social and economic impacts of any product or service offering, market intervention or other activity on an economy as a whole and on the companies, organization and individuals who are its main economic actors.
Mutation	Mutation is a permanent, sometimes transmissible (if the change is to a germ cell) change to the genetic material (usually DNA or RNA) of a cell. They can be caused by copying errors in the genetic material during cell division and by exposure to radiation, chemicals, or viruses, or can occur deliberately under cellular control during the processes such as

	meiosis or hypermutation.
Syndrome	The term syndrome is the association of several clinically recognizable features, signs, symptoms, phenomena or characteristics which often occur together, so that the presence of one feature indicates the presence of the others.
Stereotype	A stereotype is considered to be a group concept, held by one social group about another.They are often used in a negative or prejudicial sense and are frequently used to justify certain discriminatory behaviors. This allows powerful social groups to legitimize and protect their dominant position
Femininity	Femininity is the set of characteristics defined by a culture for idealized females.
Masculinity	Masculinity is a culturally determined value reflecting the set of characteristics of maleness.
Hyperactivity	Hyperactivity can be described as a state in which a individual is abnormally easily excitable and exuberant. Strong emotional reactions and a very short span of attention is also typical for the individual.
Congenital	A condition existing at birth is referred to as congenital.
Cortisol	Cortisol is a corticosteroid hormone that is involved in the response to stress; it increases blood pressure and blood sugar levels and suppresses the immune system. Synthetic cortisol, also known as hydrocortisone, is used as a drug mainly to fight allergies and inflammation.
Congenital adrenal hyperplasia	Congenital adrenal hyperplasia refers to a group of inherited disorders relating to the adrenal glands, characterized by a deficiency in the hormones cortisol and aldosterone and an overproduction of androgen. Without these hormones, steroids are 'diverted' to becoming androgens, a form of male sex hormones. This causes early (or inappropriate) appearance of male characteristics.
Bisexuality	Bisexuality is a sexual orientation characterized by aesthetic attraction, romantic love and sexual desire for both males and females.
Prenatal	Prenatal period refers to the time from conception to birth.
Theories	Theories are logically self-consistent models or frameworks describing the behavior of a certain natural or social phenomenon. They are broad explanations and predictions concerning phenomena of interest.
Castration	Castration is any action, surgical, chemical or otherwise, by which a biological male loses use of the testes. This causes sterilization, i.e. prevents him from reproducing; it also greatly reduces the production of certain hormones, such as testosterone.
Generalization	In conditioning, the tendency for a conditioned response to be evoked by stimuli that are similar to the stimulus to which the response was conditioned is a generalization. The greater the similarity among the stimuli, the greater the probability of generalization.
Ovulation	Ovulation is the process in the menstrual cycle by which a mature ovarian follicle ruptures and discharges an ovum (also known as an oocyte, female gamete, or casually, an egg) that participates in reproduction.
Motivation	In psychology, motivation is the driving force (desire) behind all actions of an organism.
Clinical study	An intensive investigation of a single person, especially one suffering from some injury or disease is referred to as a clinical study.
Correlational study	A correlational study observes or measures two or more variables to find relationships between them. Such studies can identify lawful relationships but cannot determine whether change in one variable is the cause of change in another.

Anabolic steroid	Anabolic steroids are a class of natural and synthetic steroid hormones that promote cell growth and division, resulting in growth of muscle tissue and sometimes bone size and strength. Testosterone is the best known natural anabolic steroid, as well as the best known natural androgen.
Scientific research	Research that is objective, systematic, and testable is called scientific research.
Gynecomastia	Gynecomastia is the development of abnormally large breasts on men. Gynecomastia is not simply a buildup of adipose tissue, but includes the development of glandular tissue as well.
Amenorrhea	Amenorrhea (AmE) is the absence of a menstrual period in a woman of reproductive age. Physiologic states of amenorrhea are seen during pregnancy and lactation (breastfeeding). Outside of the reproductive years there is absence of menses during childhood and after menopause.
Depression	In everyday language depression refers to any downturn in mood, which may be relatively transitory and perhaps due to something trivial. This is differentiated from Clinical depression which is marked by symptoms that last two weeks or more and are so severe that they interfere with daily living.
Tumor	A tumor is an abnormal growth that when located in the brain can either be malignant and directly destroy brain tissue, or be benign and disrupt functioning by increasing intracranial pressure.
Liver	The liver plays a major role in metabolism and has a number of functions in the body including detoxification, glycogen storage and plasma protein synthesis. It also produces bile, which is important for digestion. The liver converts most carbohydrates, proteing, and fats into glucose.
Psychotic behavior	A psychotic behavior is a severe psychological disorder characterized by hallucinations and loss of contact with reality.
Placebo	Placebo refers to a bogus treatment that has the appearance of being genuine.
Chronic	Chronic refers to a relatively long duration, usually more than a few months.
Stroke	A stroke occurs when the blood supply to a part of the brain is suddenly interrupted by occlusion, by hemorrhage, or other causes
Cognition	The intellectual processes through which information is obtained, transformed, stored, retrieved, and otherwise used is cognition.
Working Memory	Working memory is the collection of structures and processes in the brain used for temporarily storing and manipulating information. Working memory consists of both memory for items that are currently being processed, and components governing attention and directing the processing itself.
Anatomy	Anatomy is the branch of biology that deals with the structure and organization of living things. It can be divided into animal anatomy (zootomy) and plant anatomy (phytonomy). Major branches of anatomy include comparative anatomy, histology, and human anatomy.
Hull	Hull is best known for the Drive Reduction Theory which postulated that behavior occurs in response to primary drives such as hunger, thirst, sexual interest, etc. When the goal of the drive is attained the drive is reduced. This reduction of drive serves as a reinforcer for learning.
Midbrain	Located between the hindbrain and forebrain, a region in which many nerve-fiber systems ascend and descend to connect the higher and lower portions of the brain is referred to as midbrain. It is archipallian in origin, meaning its general architecture is shared with the

	most ancient of vertebrates. Dopamine produced in the subtantia nigra plays a role in motivation and habituation of species from humans to the most elementary animals such as insects.
Estrus	The estrus cycle refers to the recurring physiologic changes that are induced by reproductive hormones in most mammalian placental females (humans and great apes are the only mammals who undergo a menstrual cycle instead).
Ventromedial nucleus	Ventromedial nucleus refers to a central area on the underside of the hypothalamus that appears to function as a stop-eating center.
Sexual orientation	Sexual orientation refers to the sex or gender of people who are the focus of a person's amorous or erotic desires, fantasies, and spontaneous feelings, the gender(s) toward which one is primarily "oriented".
Homosexuality	Homosexuality refers to a sexual orientation characterized by aesthetic attraction, romantic love, and sexual desire exclusively for members of the same sex or gender identity.
Concordance	Concordance as used in genetics means the presence of the same trait in both members of a pair of twins, or in sets of individuals. A twin study examines the concordance rates of twins having the same trait, especially a disease, which can help determine how much the disease is affected by genetics versus environment.
Monozygotic	Identical twins occur when a single egg is fertilized to form one zygote, calld monozygotic, but the zygote then divides into two separate embryos. The two embryos develop into foetuses sharing the same womb. Monozygotic twins are genetically identical unless there has been a mutation in development, and they are almost always the same gender.
Dizygotic	Fraternal twins (commonly known as "non-identical twins") usually occur when two fertilized eggs are implanted in the uterine wall at the same time. The two eggs form two zygotes, and these twins are therefore also known as dizygotic.
Homosexual	Homosexual refers to a sexual orientation characterized by aesthetic attraction, romantic love, and sexual desire exclusively for members of the same sex or gender identity.
Control subjects	Control subjects are participants in an experiment who do not receive the treatment effect but for whom all other conditions are held comparable to those of experimental subjects.
Nerve	A nerve is an enclosed, cable-like bundle of nerve fibers or axons, which includes the glia that ensheath the axons in myelin. Neurons are sometimes called nerve cells, though this term is technically imprecise since many neurons do not form nerves.
Social learning	Social learning is learning that occurs as a function of observing, retaining and replicating behavior observed in others. Although social learning can occur at any stage in life, it is thought to be particularly important during childhood, particularly as authority becomes important.
Learning	Learning is a relatively permanent change in behavior that results from experience. Thus, to attribute a behavioral change to learning, the change must be relatively permanent and must result from experience.
Transsexual	A transsexual person establishes a permanent identity with the opposite gender to their assigned sex. They make or desire to make a transition from their birth sex to that of the opposite sex, with some type of medical alteration to their body.
Biopsychology	Biopsychology is the scientific study of the biological bases of behavior and mental states. Empirical experiments study changes in central nervous system activation in response to a stimulus.
Evolutionary	A perspective that focuses on how humans have evolved and adapted behaviors required for

perspective	survival against various environmental pressures over the long course is called the evolutionary perspective.
Attention	Attention is the cognitive process of selectively concentrating on one thing while ignoring other things. Psychologists have labeled three types of attention: sustained attention, selective attention, and divided attention.
Heterosexuality	Sexual attraction and behavior directed to the opposite sex is heterosexuality.

Electrode | Any device used to electrically stimulate nerve tissue or to record its activity is an electrode.

Rapid eye movement | Rapid eye movement is the stage of sleep during which the most vivid (though not all) dreams occur. During this stage, the eyes move rapidly, and the activity of the brain's neurons is quite similar to that during waking hours. It is the lightest form of sleep in that people awakened during REM usually feel alert and refreshed.

Stages | Stages represent relatively discrete periods of time in which functioning is qualitatively different from functioning at other periods.

Electroencep-alogram | Electroencephalography is the neurophysiologic measurement of the electrical activity of the brain by recording from electrodes placed on the scalp, or in the special cases on the cortex. The resulting traces are known as an electroencephalogram and represent so-called brainwaves.

Sleep spindles | Sleep spindles refer to distinctive bursts of brain-wave activity that indicate a person is asleep.

Stage 1 sleep | The state of transition between wakefulness and sleep, characterized by relatively rapid, low-voltage brain waves is called stage 1 sleep.

Stage 2 sleep | A sleep deeper than that of stage 1, characterized by a slower, more regular wave pattern, along with momentary interruptions of 'sleep spindles' is called stage 2 sleep.

Amplitude | Amplitude is a nonnegative scalar measure of a wave's magnitude of oscillation.

Stage 3 sleep | A sleep period characterized by slow brain waves, with greater peaks and valleys in the wave pattern is referred to as stage 3 sleep.

Stage 4 sleep | The deepest stage of sleep, during which we are least responsive to outside stimulation is referred to as stage 4 sleep.

Delta wave | A delta wave is a large, slow brain wave associated with deep sleep. They are present only in stage-three sleep, stage -four sleep, and coma.

Alpha wave | The brain wave associated with deep relaxation is referred to as the alpha wave. Recorded by electroencephalography (EEG) , they are synchronous and coherent (regular like sawtooth) and in the frequency range of 8 - 12 Hz. It is also called Berger's wave in memory of the founder of EEG.

Rem sleep | Sleep characterized by rapid eye movements, paralysis of large muscles, fast and irregular heart rate and respiration rate, increased brain-wave activity, and vivid dreams is referred to as REM sleep. An infant spends about half the time in REM sleep when sleeping.

Nervous system | The body's electrochemical communication circuitry, made up of billions of neurons is a nervous system.

Brain | The brain controls and coordinates most movement, behavior and homeostatic body functions such as heartbeat, blood pressure, fluid balance and body temperature. Functions of the brain are responsible for cognition, emotion, memory, motor learning and other sorts of learning. The brain is primarily made up of two types of cells: glia and neurons.

Autonomic nervous system | A division of the peripheral nervous system, the autonomic nervous system, regulates glands and activities such as heartbeat, respiration, digestion, and dilation of the pupils. It is responsible for homeostasis, maintaining a relatively constant internal environment .

Emotion | An emotion is a mental states that arise spontaneously, rather than through conscious effort. They are often accompanied by physiological changes.

Correlation | A statistical technique for determining the degree of association between two or more

	variables is referred to as correlation.
Somnambulism	Sleepwalking that occurs during a partial arousal from Stage 4 sleep is referred to as somnambulism.
The Interpretation of Dreams	The Interpretation of Dreams is a book by Sigmund Freud. The book introduces the Id, the Ego, and the Superego, and describes Freud's theory of the unconscious with respect to Dream interpretation. Widely considered to be his most important contribution to Psychology.
Cerebral cortex	The cerebral cortex is the outermost layer of the cerebrum and has a grey color. It is made up of four lobes and it is involved in many complex brain functions including memory, perceptual awareness, "thinking", language and consciousness. The cerebral cortex receives sensory information from many different sensory organs eg: eyes, ears, etc. and processes the information.
Consciousness	The awareness of the sensations, thoughts, and feelings being experienced at a given moment is called consciousness.
Lucid dream	A dream during which the dreamer is aware of dreaming and is often able to influence the content of the dream while it is in progress is a lucid dream.
Theories	Theories are logically self-consistent models or frameworks describing the behavior of a certain natural or social phenomenon. They are broad explanations and predictions concerning phenomena of interest.
Homeostasis	Homeostasis is the property of an open system, especially living organisms, to regulate its internal environment so as to maintain a stable condition, by means of multiple dynamic equilibrium adjustments controlled by interrelated regulation mechanisms.
Motivation	In psychology, motivation is the driving force (desire) behind all actions of an organism.
Metaphor	A metaphor is a rhetorical trope where a comparison is made between two seemingly unrelated subjects
Species	Species refers to a reproductively isolated breeding population.
Nocturnal	A person who exhibits nocturnal habits is referred to as a night owl.
Biological needs	Beyond physiological needs for survivial, the next level are motivations that have an obvious biological basis but are not required for the immediate survival of the organism. These biological needs include the powerful motivations for sex, parenting and aggression.
Circadian rhythm	The circadian rhythm is a name given to the "internal body clock" that regulates the (roughly) 24 hour cycle of biological processes in animals and plants.
Society	The social sciences use the term society to mean a group of people that form a semi-closed (or semi-open) social system, in which most interactions are with other individuals belonging to the group.
Deprivation	Deprivation, is the loss or withholding of normal stimulation, nutrition, comfort, love, and so forth; a condition of lacking. The level of stimulation is less than what is required.
Premise	A premise is a statement presumed true within the context of a discourse, especially of a logical argument.
Case study	A carefully drawn biography that may be obtained through interviews, questionnaires, and psychological tests is called a case study.
Cognition	The intellectual processes through which information is obtained, transformed, stored, retrieved, and otherwise used is cognition.
Microsleep	A microsleep is a period of sleep lasting a few seconds. It often occurs as a result of a

	sleep debt or mental fatigue.
Creativity	Creativity is the ability to think about something in novel and unusual ways and come up with unique solutions to problems. It involves divergent thinking, having many solutions or views to a problem.
IQ test	An IQ test is a standardized test developed to measure a person's cognitive abilities ("intelligence") in relation to their age group.
Physiological changes	Alterations in heart rate, blood pressure, perspiration, and other involuntary responses are physiological changes.
Intelligence test	An intelligence test is a standardized means of assessing a person's current mental ability, for example, the Stanford-Binet test and the Wechsler Adult Intelligence Scale.
Antidepressant	An antidepressant is a medication used primarily in the treatment of clinical depression. They are not thought to produce tolerance, although sudden withdrawal may produce adverse effects. They create little if any immediate change in mood and require between several days and several weeks to take effect.
Tricyclic	Tricyclic antidepressants are a class of antidepressant drugs first used in the 1950s. They are named after the drugs' molecular structure, which contains three rings of atoms.
Tricyclic antidepressant	A tricyclic antidepressant is of a class of antidepressant drugs first used in the 1950s. They are named after the drugs' molecular structure, which contains three rings of atoms.
Depression	In everyday language depression refers to any downturn in mood, which may be relatively transitory and perhaps due to something trivial. This is differentiated from Clinical depression which is marked by symptoms that last two weeks or more and are so severe that they interfere with daily living.
Antidepressants	Antidepressants are medications used primarily in the treatment of clinical depression. Antidepressants create little if any immediate change in mood and require between several days and several weeks to take effect.
Rem rebound	Rem rebound refers to the increased amount of REM sleep that occurs after REM deprivation; often associated with unpleasant dreams or nightmares.
Neuroscience	A field that combines the work of psychologists, biologists, biochemists, medical researchers, and others in the study of the structure and function of the nervous system is neuroscience.
Hypothalamus	The hypothalamus is a region of the brain located below the thalamus, forming the major portion of the ventral region of the diencephalon and functioning to regulate certain metabolic processes and other autonomic activities.
Neurologist	A physician who studies the nervous system, especially its structure, functions, and abnormalities is referred to as neurologist.
Midbrain	Located between the hindbrain and forebrain, a region in which many nerve-fiber systems ascend and descend to connect the higher and lower portions of the brain is referred to as midbrain. It is archipallian in origin, meaning its general architecture is shared with the most ancient of vertebrates. Dopamine produced in the subtantia nigra plays a role in motivation and habituation of species from humans to the most elementary animals such as insects.
Lesion	A lesion is a non-specific term referring to abnormal tissue in the body. It can be caused by any disease process including trauma (physical, chemical, electrical), infection, neoplasm, metabolic and autoimmune.
Reticular	The reticular activating system is the part of the brain believed to be the center of arousal

activating system	and motivation. It is situated between the brain stem and the central nervous system (CNS).
Brain stem	The brain stem is the stalk of the brain below the cerebral hemispheres. It is the major route for communication between the forebrain and the spinal cord and peripheral nerves. It also controls various functions including respiration, regulation of heart rhythms, and primary aspects of sound localization.
Reticular formation	Reticular formation is a part of the brain which is involved in stereotypical actions, such as walking, sleeping, and lying down. The reticular formation, phylogenetically one of the oldest portions of the brain, is a poorly-differentiated area of the brain stem.
Forebrain	The forebrain is the highest level of the brain. Key structures in the forebrain are the limbic system, thalamus, basal ganglia, hypothalamus, and cerebral cortex.
Optic chiasm	Optic chiasm refers to the point at which the optic nerves from the inside half of each eye cross over and then project to the opposite half of the brain.
Optic tract	The optic tract is a part of the visual system in the brain. It is a continuation of the optic nerve and runs from the optic chiasm (where half of the information from each eye crosses sides, and half stays on the same side) to the lateral geniculate nucleus.
Optic nerve	The optic nerve is the nerve that transmits visual information from the retina to the brain. The optic nerve is composed of retinal ganglion cell axons and support cells.
Nerve	A nerve is an enclosed, cable-like bundle of nerve fibers or axons, which includes the glia that ensheath the axons in myelin. Neurons are sometimes called nerve cells, though this term is technically imprecise since many neurons do not form nerves.
Cones	Cones are photoreceptors that transmit sensations of color, function in bright light, and used in visual acutity. Infants prior to months of age can only distinguish green and red indicating the cones are not fully developed; they can see all of the colors by 2 months of
Rods	Rods are cylindrical shaped photoreceptors that are sensitive to the intensity of light. Rods require less light to function than cone cells, and therefore are the primary source of visual information at night.
Neuron	The neuron is the primary cell of the nervous system. They are found in the brain, the spinal cord, in the nerves and ganglia of the peripheral nervous system. It is a specialized cell that conducts impulses through the nervous system and contains three major parts: cell body, dendrites, and an axon. It can have many dendrites but only one axon.
Retina	The retina is a thin layer of cells at the back of the eyeball. It is the part of the eye which converts light into nervous signals. The retina contains photoreceptor cells which receive the light; the resulting neural signals then undergo complex processing by other neurons of the retina, and are transformed into action potentials in retinal ganglion cells whose axons form the optic nerve.
Receptor	A sensory receptor is a structure that recognizes a stimulus in the internal or external environment of an organism. In response to stimuli the sensory receptor initiates sensory transduction by creating graded potentials or action potentials in the same cell or in an adjacent one.
Nucleus	In neuroanatomy, a cluster of cell bodies of neurons within the central nervous system is a nucleus.
Genetics	Genetics is the science of genes, heredity, and the variation of organisms.
Mutation	Mutation is a permanent, sometimes transmissible (if the change is to a germ cell) change to the genetic material (usually DNA or RNA) of a cell. They can be caused by copying errors in

	the genetic material during cell division and by exposure to radiation, chemicals, or viruses, or can occur deliberately under cellular control during the processes such as meiosis or hypermutation.
Gene	A gene is an ultramicroscopic area of the chromosome. It is the smallest physical unit of the DNA molecule that carries a piece of hereditary information.
Protein	A protein is a complex, high-molecular-weight organic compound that consists of amino acids joined by peptide bonds. It is essential to the structure and function of all living cells and viruses. Many are enzymes or subunits of enzymes.
Affect	A subjective feeling or emotional tone often accompanied by bodily expressions noticeable to others is called affect.
Melatonin	Melatonin produced in the pineal gland acts as an endocrine hormone since it is released into the blood. Melatonin helps regulate sleep-wake or circadian rhythms.
Anxiety	Anxiety is a complex combination of the feeling of fear, apprehension and worry often accompanied by physical sensations such as palpitations, chest pain and/or shortness of breath.
Benzodiazepines	The benzodiazepines are a class of drugs with hypnotic, anxiolytic, anticonvulsant, amnestic and muscle relaxant properties. Benzodiazepines are often used for short-term relief of severe, disabling anxiety or insomnia.
Chronic	Chronic refers to a relatively long duration, usually more than a few months.
Serotonin	Serotonin, a neurotransmitter, is believed to play an important part of the biochemistry of depression, bipolar disorder and anxiety. It is also believed to be influential on sexuality and appetite.
Amphetamine	Amphetamine is a synthetic stimulant used to suppress the appetite, control weight, and treat disorders including narcolepsy and ADHD. It is also used recreationally and for performance enhancement.
Stimulant	A stimulant is a drug which increases the activity of the sympathetic nervous system and produces a sense of euphoria or awakeness.
Insomnia	Insomnia is a sleep disorder characterized by an inability to sleep and/or to remain asleep for a reasonable period during the night.
Cocaine	Cocaine is a crystalline tropane alkaloid that is obtained from the leaves of the coca plant. It is a stimulant of the central nervous system and an appetite suppressant, creating what has been described as a euphoric sense of happiness and increased energy.
Norepinephrine	Norepinephrine is released from the adrenal glands as a hormone into the blood, but it is also a neurotransmitter in the nervous system. As a stress hormone, it affects parts of the human brain where attention and impulsivity are controlled. Along with epinephrine, this compound effects the fight-or-flight response, activating the sympathetic nervous system to directly increase heart rate, release energy from fat, and increase muscle readiness.
Catecholamines	Catecholamines are chemical compounds derived from the amino acid tyrosine that act as hormones or neurotransmitters. High catecholamine levels in blood are associated with stress.
Reuptake	Reuptake is the reabsorption of a neurotransmitter by the molecular transporter of a pre-synaptic neuron after it has performed its function of transmitting a neural impulse.
Dopamine	Dopamine is critical to the way the brain controls our movements and is a crucial part of the basal ganglia motor loop. It is commonly associated with the 'pleasure system' of the brain, providing feelings of enjoyment and reinforcement to motivate us to do, or continue doing, certain activities.

Blocking	If the one of the two members of a compound stimulus fails to produce the CR due to an earlier conditioning of the other member of the compound stimulus, blocking has occurred.
Synapse	A synapse is specialized junction through which cells of the nervous system signal to one another and to non-neuronal cells such as muscles or glands.
Pineal gland	The pineal gland is a small endocrine gland. It is located near the center of the brain, between the two hemispheres and near the central switching point of the thalamic bodies. It is responsible for the production of melatonin, which has a role in regulating circadian rhythms.
Gland	A gland is an organ in an animal's body that synthesizes a substance for release such as hormones, often into the bloodstream or into cavities inside the body or its outer surface.
Puberty	Puberty refers to the process of physical changes by which a child's body becomes an adult body capable of reproduction.
Exogenous	Exogenous refers to an action or object coming from outside a system.
Hypersomnia	Hypersomnia is an excessive amount of sleepiness, resulting in an inability to stay awake. A person is considered to have hypersomnia if he or she sleeps more than 10 hours per day on a regular basis for at least two weeks.
Withdrawal symptoms	Withdrawal symptoms are physiological changes that occur when the use of a drug is stopped or dosage decreased.
Habit	A habit is a response that has become completely separated from its eliciting stimulus. Early learning theorists used the term to describe S-R associations, however not all S-R associations become a habit, rather many are extinguished after reinforcement is withdrawn.
Sleep apnea	Sleep apnea refers to a sleep disorder involving periods during sleep when breathing stops and the person must awaken briefly in order to breathe; major symptoms are excessive daytime sleepiness and loud snoring.
Apnea	Apnea is the absence of external breathing. During apnea there is no movement of the muscles of respiration and the volume of the lungs initially remains unchanged. .
Nocturnal myoclonus	Nocturnal myoclonus, is a sleep disorder where the patient moves involuntarily during sleep. It can range from a small amount in the ankles and toes to wild flailing of all four limbs.
Latency	In child development, latency refers to a phase of psychosexual development characterized by repression of sexual impulses. In learning theory, latency is the delay between stimulus (S) and response (R), which according to Hull depends on the strength of the association.
Narcolepsy	A serious sleep disorder characterized by excessive daytime sleepiness and sudden, uncontrollable attacks of REM sleep is called narcolepsy.
Cataplexy	Sudden loss of muscle tone that accompanies narcolepsy is called cataplexy.
Hallucination	A hallucination is a sensory perception experienced in the absence of an external stimulus, as distinct from an illusion, which is a misperception of an external stimulus. They may occur in any sensory modality - visual, auditory, olfactory, gustatory, tactile, or mixed.
Hypnagogic	When in a hypnagogic state a person can have lifelike auditory, visual, or tactile hallucinations, perhaps even accompanied by full body paralysis. The individual is aware that these are hallucinations; the frightening part, in many cases, is the inability to react to them, even being unable to make a sound. In other cases one may enjoy truly vivid imaginations.
Orexin	Orexin is the common name given to a pair of highly excititory neuropeptide hormones that were simultaneously discovered by two groups of reseachers in rat brains. The University of

	Texas, coined the term orexin to reflect the appetite-stimulating activity of these hormones.
Coding	In senation, coding is the process by which information about the quality and quantity of a stimulus is preserved in the pattern of action potentials sent through sensory neurons to the central nervous system.
Sleep cycle	Sleep cycle refers to a cycle of sleep lasting about 90 minutes and including one or more stages of NREM sleep followed by a period of REM sleep.
Polyphasic sleep	Polyphasic sleep is pattern specification intended to compress sleep time to 2-5 hours daily. This is achieved by spreading out sleep into short (around 20-45 minute) naps throughout the
Pinel	Pinel is regarded as the father of modern psychiatry. He was a clinician believing that medical truth derived from clinical experience. While at Bicêtre, Pinel did away with bleeding, purging, and blistering in favor a therapy that involved close contact with and careful observation of patients.
Bias	A bias is a prejudice in a general or specific sense, usually in the sense for having a preference to one particular point of view or ideological perspective.
Physiology	The study of the functions and activities of living cells, tissues, and organs and of the physical and chemical phenomena involved is referred to as physiology.

Drug addiction	Drug addiction, or substance dependence is the compulsive use of drugs, to the point where the user has no effective choice but to continue use.
Addiction	Addiction is an uncontrollable compulsion to repeat a behavior regardless of its consequences. Many drugs or behaviors can precipitate a pattern of conditions recognized as addiction, which include a craving for more of the drug or behavior, increased physiological tolerance to exposure, and withdrawal symptoms in the absence of the stimulus.
Metabolites	Metabolites are the intermediates and products of metabolism.
Brain	The brain controls and coordinates most movement, behavior and homeostatic body functions such as heartbeat, blood pressure, fluid balance and body temperature. Functions of the brain are responsible for cognition, emotion, memory, motor learning and other sorts of learning. The brain is primarily made up of two types of cells: glia and neurons.
Capillary	The capillary is the smallest of a body's blood vessels, measuring 5-10 ìm. They connect arteries and veins, and most closely interact with tissues.
Lungs	The lungs are the essential organs of respiration. Its principal function is to transport oxygen from the atmosphere into the bloodstream, and excrete carbon dioxide from the bloodstream into the atmosphere.
Marijuana	Marijuana is the dried vegetable matter of the Cannabis sativa plant. It contains large concentrations of compounds that have medicinal and psychoactive effects when consumed, usually by smoking or eating.
Cocaine	Cocaine is a crystalline tropane alkaloid that is obtained from the leaves of the coca plant. It is a stimulant of the central nervous system and an appetite suppressant, creating what has been described as a euphoric sense of happiness and increased energy.
Nervous system	The body's electrochemical communication circuitry, made up of billions of neurons is a nervous system.
Central nervous system	The vertebrate central nervous system consists of the brain and spinal cord.
Neuron	The neuron is the primary cell of the nervous system. They are found in the brain, the spinal cord, in the nerves and ganglia of the peripheral nervous system. It is a specialized cell that conducts impulses through the nervous system and contains three major parts: cell body, dendrites, and an axon. It can have many dendrites but only one axon.
Metabolism	Metabolism is the biochemical modification of chemical compounds in living organisms and cells.
Receptor	A sensory receptor is a structure that recognizes a stimulus in the internal or external environment of an organism. In response to stimuli the sensory receptor initiates sensory transduction by creating graded potentials or action potentials in the same cell or in an adjacent one.
Enzyme	An enzyme is a protein that catalyzes, or speeds up, a chemical reaction. Enzymes are essential to sustain life because most chemical reactions in biological cells would occur too slowly, or would lead to different products, without enzymes.
Liver	The liver plays a major role in metabolism and has a number of functions in the body including detoxification, glycogen storage and plasma protein synthesis. It also produces bile, which is important for digestion. The liver converts most carbohydrates, proteing, and fats into glucose.
Psychoactive drug	A psychoactive drug or psychotropic substance is a chemical that alters brain function, resulting in temporary changes in perception, mood, consciousness, or behavior. Such drugs

	are often used for recreational and spiritual purposes, as well as in medicine, especially for treating neurological and psychological illnesses.
Neurotransmitter	A neurotransmitter is a chemical that is used to relay, amplify and modulate electrical signals between a neurons and another cell.
Drug tolerance	Drug tolerance occurs when a subject's reaction to a drug (such as a painkiller or intoxicant) decreases so that larger doses are required to achieve the same effect. In addicted patients, the resulting pattern of uncontrolled escalating doses may lead to drug overdose.
Syndrome	The term syndrome is the association of several clinically recognizable features, signs, symptoms, phenomena or characteristics which often occur together, so that the presence of one feature indicates the presence of the others.
Physical dependence	Physical dependence describes increased tolerance of a drug combined with a physical need of the drug to function. Abrupt cessation of the drug is typically associated with negative physical withdrawal symptoms. Physical dependence is distinguished from addiction. While addiction tends to describe psychological and behavioral attributes, physical dependence is defined primarily using physical and biological concepts.
Withdrawal effects	Withdrawal effects refer to the physiological, mental, and behavioral disturbances that can occur when a long-term user of a drug stops taking the drug.
Withdrawal symptoms	Withdrawal symptoms are physiological changes that occur when the use of a drug is stopped or dosage decreased.
Adaptation	Adaptation is a lowering of sensitivity to a stimulus following prolonged exposure to that stimulus. Behavioral adaptations are special ways a particular organism behaves to survive in its natural habitat.
Neural adaptation	Neural adaptation refers to a temporary change of the neural response to a stimulus as the result of preceding stimulation.
Learning	Learning is a relatively permanent change in behavior that results from experience. Thus, to attribute a behavioral change to learning, the change must be relatively permanent and must result from experience.
Psychological dependence	Psychological dependence may lead to psychological withdrawal symptoms. Addictions can theoretically form for any rewarding behavior, or as a habitual means to avoid undesired activity, but typically they only do so to a clinical level in individuals who have emotional, social, or psychological dysfunctions, taking the place of normal positive stimuli not otherwise attained
Amygdala	Located in the brain's medial temporal lobe, the almond-shaped amygdala is believed to play a key role in the emotions. It forms part of the limbic system and is linked to both fear responses and pleasure. Its size is positively correlated with aggressive behavior across species.
Species	Species refers to a reproductively isolated breeding population.
Hypothesis	A specific statement about behavior or mental processes that is testable through research is a hypothesis.
Heroin	Heroin is widely and illegally used as a powerful and addictive drug producing intense euphoria, which often disappears with increasing tolerance. Heroin is a semi-synthetic opioid. It is the 3,6-diacetyl derivative of morphine and is synthesised from it by acetylation.
Conditioning	Conditioning describes the process by which behaviors can be learned or modified through

	interaction with the environment.
Pavlovian conditioning	Pavlovian conditioning, synonymous with classical conditioning is a type of learning found in animals, caused by the association (or pairing) of two stimuli or what Ivan Pavlov described as the learning of conditional behavior, therefore called conditioning.
Conditional response	A conditional response is elicited by a conditional stimulus in a conditional reflex.
Conditioned compensatory response	A homeostatic response that counteracts a drug's effect after repeated exposures is a conditioned compensatory response.
Sensitization	Sensitization is a process whereby an organism is made more responsive to certain aspects of its environment. For example, increases in the effects of a drug as a result of repeated administration. Also known as reverse tolerance.
Amphetamine	Amphetamine is a synthetic stimulant used to suppress the appetite, control weight, and treat disorders including narcolepsy and ADHD. It is also used recreationally and for performance enhancement.
Stimulant	A stimulant is a drug which increases the activity of the sympathetic nervous system and produces a sense of euphoria or awakeness.
Sullivan	Sullivan developed the Self System, a configuration of the personality traits developed in childhood and reinforced by positive affirmation and the security operations developed in childhood to avoid anxiety and threats to self-esteem.
Morphine	Morphine, the principal active agent in opium, is a powerful opioid analgesic drug. According to recent research, it may also be produced naturally by the human brain. Morphine is usually highly addictive, and tolerance and physical and psychological dependence develop quickly.
Stimulus	A change in an environmental condition that elicits a response is a stimulus.
Nicotine	Nicotine is an organic compound, an alkaloid found naturally throughout the tobacco plant, with a high concentration in the leaves. It is a potent nerve poison and is included in many insecticides. In lower concentrations, the substance is a stimulant and is one of the main factors leading to the pleasure and habit-forming qualities of tobacco smoking.
Twin study	A twin study is a kind of genetic study done to determine heritability. The premise is that since identical twins (especially identical twins raised apart) have identical genotypes, differences between them are solely due to environmental factors. By examining the degree to which twins are differentiated, a study may determine the extent to which a particular trait is influenced by genes or the environment.
Heritability	Heritability It is that proportion of the observed variation in a particular phenotype within a particular population, that can be attributed to the contribution of genotype. In other words: it measures the extent to which differences between individuals in a population are due their being different genetically.
Chronic	Chronic refers to a relatively long duration, usually more than a few months.
Pancreas	The pancreas is a retroperitoneal organ that serves two functions: it produces juice containing digestive enzymes; and it produces several important hormones including insulin, glucagon, and several other hormones.
Larynx	The larynx, or voicebox, is an organ in the neck of mammals involved in protection of the trachea and sound production. The larynx houses the vocal cords, and is situated at the point where the upper tract splits into the trachea and the esophagus.
Stroke	A stroke occurs when the blood supply to a part of the brain is suddenly interrupted by

	occlusion, by hemorrhage, or other causes
Cardiovascular disease	Cardiovascular disease refers to afflictions in the mechanisms, including the heart, blood vessels, and their controllers, that are responsible for transporting blood to the body's tissues and organs. Psychological factors may play important roles in such diseases and their treatments.
Depressant	A depressant is a chemical agent that diminishes a body function or activity. The term is used in particular with regard to the central nervous system where these chemicals are known as neurotransmitters. They tend to act on the CNS by increasing the activity of a particular neurotransmitter known as gamma-aminobutyric acid (GABA).
Depression	In everyday language depression refers to any downturn in mood, which may be relatively transitory and perhaps due to something trivial. This is differentiated from Clinical depression which is marked by symptoms that last two weeks or more and are so severe that they interfere with daily living.
Addictive drugs	Addictive drugs produce a biological or psychological dependence in the user; withdrawal from them leads to a craving for the drug that in some cases can be nearly irresistible.
Hallucination	A hallucination is a sensory perception experienced in the absence of an external stimulus, as distinct from an illusion, which is a misperception of an external stimulus. They may occur in any sensory modality - visual, auditory, olfactory, gustatory, tactile, or mixed.
Tremor	Tremor is the rhythmic, oscillating shaking movement of the whole body or just a certain part of it, caused by problems of the neurons responsible from muscle action.
Cirrhosis	Cirrhosis is a chronic disease of the liver in which liver tissue is replaced by connective tissue, resulting in the loss of liver function. Cirrhosis is caused by damage from toxins (including alcohol), metabolic problems, chronic viral hepatitis or other causes
Dementia	Dementia is progressive decline in cognitive function due to damage or disease in the brain beyond what might be expected from normal aging.
Affect	A subjective feeling or emotional tone often accompanied by bodily expressions noticeable to others is called affect.
Fetus	A fetus develops from the end of the 8th week of pregnancy (when the major structures have formed), until birth.
Apoptosis	Apoptosis is one of the main types of programmed cell death. As such, it is a process of deliberate suicide by an unwanted cell in a multicellular organism.
Gastrointest-nal tract	The gastrointestinal tract is the system of organs within multicellular animals which takes in food, digests it to extract energy and nutrients, and expels the remaining waste.
Cannabinoids	Family of chemicals in marijuana believed to be responsible for its mood- and behavior-altering ability are called cannabinoids.
Hashish	Hashish is a psychoactive drug derived from the Cannabis plant. It is used for its relaxing and mind-altering effects.
Cannabis	The hemp plant from which marijuana, hashish, and THC are derived is the cannabis.
Population	Population refers to all members of a well-defined group of organisms, events, or things.
Punishment	Punishment is the addtion of a stimulus that reduces the frequency of a response, or the removal of a stimulus that results in a reduction of the response.
Narcotic	The term narcotic originally referred to a variety of substances that induced sleep (such state is narcosis). In legal context, narcotic refers to opium, opium derivatives, and their semisynthetic or totally synthetic substitutes.

Opiates	A group of narcotics derived from the opium poppy that provide a euphoric rush and depress the nervous system are referred to as opiates.
Perception	Perception is the process of acquiring, interpreting, selecting, and organizing sensory information.
Consciousness	The awareness of the sensations, thoughts, and feelings being experienced at a given moment is called consciousness.
Glaucoma	Glaucoma is a group of diseases of the optic nerve involving loss of retinal ganglion cells. Untreated glaucoma leads to permanent damage of the optic nerve and resultant visual field loss, which can progress to blindness.
Seizure	A seizure is a temporary alteration in brain function expressed as a changed mental state, tonic or clonic movements and various other symptoms. They are due to temporary abnormal electrical activity of a group of brain cells.
Local anesthetic	Local anesthetic drugs act mainly by inhibiting sodium influx through sodium-specific ion channels in the neuronal cell membrane, in particular the so-called voltage-gated sodium channels. When the influx of sodium is interrupted, an action potential cannot arise and signal conduction is thus inhibited.
Psychotic behavior	A psychotic behavior is a severe psychological disorder characterized by hallucinations and loss of contact with reality.
Psychosis	Psychosis is a generic term for mental states in which the components of rational thought and perception are severely impaired. Persons experiencing a psychosis may experience hallucinations, hold paranoid or delusional beliefs, demonstrate personality changes and exhibit disorganized thinking. This is usually accompanied by features such as a lack of insight into the unusual or bizarre nature of their behavior, difficulties with social interaction and impairments in carrying out the activities of daily living.
Schizophrenia	Schizophrenia is characterized by persistent defects in the perception or expression of reality. A person suffering from untreated schizophrenia typically demonstrates grossly disorganized thinking, and may also experience delusions or auditory hallucinations
Paranoid	The term paranoid is typically used in a general sense to signify any self-referential delusion, or more specifically, to signify a delusion involving the fear of persecution.
Paranoid schizophrenia	Paranoid schizophrenia is a type of schizophrenia characterized primarily by delusions-commonly of persecution-and by vivid hallucinations .
Insomnia	Insomnia is a sleep disorder characterized by an inability to sleep and/or to remain asleep for a reasonable period during the night.
Epinephrine	Epinephrine is a hormone and a neurotransmitter. Epinephrine plays a central role in the short-term stress reaction—the physiological response to threatening or exciting conditions. It is secreted by the adrenal medulla. When released into the bloodstream, epinephrine binds to multiple receptors and has numerous effects throughout the body.
Norepinephrine	Norepinephrine is released from the adrenal glands as a hormone into the blood, but it is also a neurotransmitter in the nervous system. As a stress hormone, it affects parts of the human brain where attention and impulsivity are controlled. Along with epinephrine, this compound effects the fight-or-flight response, activating the sympathetic nervous system to directly increase heart rate, release energy from fat, and increase muscle readiness.
Catecholamines	Catecholamines are chemical compounds derived from the amino acid tyrosine that act as hormones or neurotransmitters. High catecholamine levels in blood are associated with stress.
Reuptake	Reuptake is the reabsorption of a neurotransmitter by the molecular transporter of a pre-

	synaptic neuron after it has performed its function of transmitting a neural impulse.
Dopamine	Dopamine is critical to the way the brain controls our movements and is a crucial part of the basal ganglia motor loop. It is commonly associated with the 'pleasure system' of the brain, providing feelings of enjoyment and reinforcement to motivate us to do, or continue doing, certain activities.
Blocking	If the one of the two members of a compound stimulus fails to produce the CR due to an earlier conditioning of the other member of the compound stimulus, blocking has occurred.
Amphetamine psychosis	Amphetamine psychosis is a form of psychosis which can result from amphetamine or methamphetamine use. Typically it appears after large doses or chronic use, although in rare cases some people may become psychotic after relatively small doses.
Ecstasy	Ecstasy as an emotion is to be outside oneself, in a trancelike state in which an individual transcends ordinary consciousness and as a result has a heightened capacity for exceptional thought or experience. Ecstasy also refers to a relatively new hallucinogen that is chemically similar to mescaline and the amphetamines.
MDMA	MDMA, most commonly known today by the street name ecstasy, is a synthetic entactogen of the phenethylamine family whose primary effect is to stimulate the secretion of large amounts of serotonin as well as dopamine and noradrenaline in the brain, causing a general sense of openness, empathy, energy, euphoria, and well-being.
Correlational study	A correlational study observes or measures two or more variables to find relationships between them. Such studies can identify lawful relationships but cannot determine whether change in one variable is the cause of change in another.
IQ test	An IQ test is a standardized test developed to measure a person's cognitive abilities ("intelligence") in relation to their age group.
Opium	Opium is a narcotic analgesic drug which is obtained from the unripe seed pods of the opium poppy. Regular use, even for a few days, invariably leads to physical tolerance and dependence. Various degrees of psychological addiction can occur, though this is relatively rare when opioids are properly used..
Codeine	Codeine is an opioid used for its analgesic, antitussive and antidiarrheal properties
Motivation	In psychology, motivation is the driving force (desire) behind all actions of an organism.
Libido	Sigmund Freud suggested that libido is the instinctual energy or force that can come into conflict with the conventions of civilized behavior. Jung, condidered the libido as the free creative, or psychic, energy an individual has to put toward personal development, or individuation.
Pupil	In the eye, the pupil is the opening in the middle of the iris. It appears black because most of the light entering it is absorbed by the tissues inside the eye. The size of the pupil is controlled by involuntary contraction and dilation of the iris, in order to regulate the intensity of light entering the eye. This is known as the pupillary reflex.
Stages	Stages represent relatively discrete periods of time in which functioning is qualitatively different from functioning at other periods.
Habit	A habit is a response that has become completely separated from its eliciting stimulus. Early learning theorists used the term to describe S-R associations, however not all S-R associations become a habit, rather many are extinguished after reinforcement is withdrawn.
Delirium	Delirium is a medical term used to describe an acute decline in attention and cognition. Delirium is probably the single most common acute disorder affecting adults in general hospitals. It affects 10-20% of all adults in hospital, and 30-40% of older patients.

Barbiturate A barbiturate is a drug that acts as a central nervous system (CNS) depressant, and by virtue of this produces a wide spectrum of effects, from mild sedation to anesthesia.

Opiate receptor Any of various cell membrane receptors that can bind with morphine and other opiates is an opiate receptor. Concentrations of such receptors are especially high in regions of the brain having pain-related functions.

Endorphin An endorphin is an endogenous opioid biochemical compound. They are peptides produced by the pituitary gland and the hypothalamus, and they resemble the opiates in their abilities to produce analgesia and a sense of well-being. In other words, they work as "natural pain killers."

Methadone Methadone is a synthetic heroin substitute used for treating heroin addicts that acts as a substitute for heroin by eliminating its effects and the craving for it. Just like heroin, tolerance and dependence frequently develop.

Society The social sciences use the term society to mean a group of people that form a semi-closed (or semi-open) social system, in which most interactions are with other individuals belonging to the group.

Survey A method of scientific investigation in which a large sample of people answer questions about their attitudes or behavior is referred to as a survey.

Biopsychology Biopsychology is the scientific study of the biological bases of behavior and mental states. Empirical experiments study changes in central nervous system activation in response to a stimulus.

Malnutrition Malnutrition is a general term for the medical condition in a person or animal caused by an unbalanced diet—either too little or too much food, or a diet missing one or more important nutrients.

Theories Theories are logically self-consistent models or frameworks describing the behavior of a certain natural or social phenomenon. They are broad explanations and predictions concerning phenomena of interest.

Detoxification Detoxification in general is the removal of toxic substances from the body. It is one of the functions of the liver and kidneys, but can also be achieved artificially by techniques such as dialysis and (in a very limited number of cases) chelation therapy.

Incentive An incentive is what is expected once a behavior is performed. An incentive acts as a reinforcer.

Pleasure center Olds and Milner discovered that electrical stimulation of a particular region in the Mesolimbic dopamine system was highly rewarding to rats; they believed they had discovered the pleasure center in the brain. It now appears that stimulation of many regions of the mesolimbic system can lead to rewarding effects--the key is that dopamine ultimately reaches neurons in the nucleus accumbens, a limbic system structure.

Priming A phenomenon in which exposure to a word or concept later makes it easier to recall related information, even when one has no conscious memory of the word or concept is called priming.

Reinforcer In operant conditioning, a reinforcer is any stimulus that increases the probability that a preceding behavior will occur again. In Classical Conditioning, the unconditioned stimulus (US) is the reinforcer.

Natural reinforcer A natural reinforcer is a stimulus that increases the probability of behavior and is a natural consequence of performing the behavior.

Mesencephalon The mesencephalon is archipallian in origin, meaning its general architecture is shared with the most ancient of vertebrates. Dopamine produced in the subtantia nigra plays a role in

	motivation and habituation of species from humans to the most elementary animals such as insects.
Midbrain	Located between the hindbrain and forebrain, a region in which many nerve-fiber systems ascend and descend to connect the higher and lower portions of the brain is referred to as midbrain. It is archipallian in origin, meaning its general architecture is shared with the most ancient of vertebrates. Dopamine produced in the subtantia nigra plays a role in motivation and habituation of species from humans to the most elementary animals such as insects.
Ventral tegmental area	The ventral tegmental area is part of the midbrain, lying close to the substantia nigra and the red nucleus. It is rich in dopamine and serotonin neurons. It is considered to be part of the pleasure or reward system, one of the major sources of incentive and behavioral motivation.
Substantia nigra	The substantia nigra is a portion of the midbrain thought to be involved in certain aspects of movement and attention. Degeneration of cells in this region is the principle pathology that underlies Parkinson's disease.
Neocortex	The neocortex is part of the cerebral cortex which covers most of the surface of the cerebral hemispheres including the frontal, parietal, occipital, and temporal lobes. Often seen as the hallmark of human intelligence, the role of this structure in the brain appears to be involved in conscious thought, spatial reasoning, and sensory perception.
Nucleus	In neuroanatomy, a cluster of cell bodies of neurons within the central nervous system is a nucleus.
Axon	An axon, or "nerve fiber," is a long slender projection of a nerve cell, or "neuron," which conducts electrical impulses away from the neuron's cell body or soma.
Nucleus accumbens	A complex of neurons that is part of the brain's "pleasure pathway" responsible for the experience of reward is referred to as the nucleus accumbens.
Lesion	A lesion is a non-specific term referring to abnormal tissue in the body. It can be caused by any disease process including trauma (physical, chemical, electrical), infection, neoplasm, metabolic and autoimmune.
Ion	An ion is an atom or group of atoms with a net electric charge. The energy required to detach an electron in its lowest energy state from an atom or molecule of a gas with less net electric charge is called the ionization potential, or ionization energy.
Incentive value	The value of a goal above and beyond its ability to fill a need is its incentive value.
Paradigm	Paradigm refers to the set of practices that defines a scientific discipline during a particular period of time. It provides a framework from which to conduct research, it ensures that a certain range of phenomena, those on which the paradigm focuses, are explored thoroughly. Itmay also blind scientists to other, perhaps more fruitful, ways of dealing with their subject matter.
Synaptic cleft	Synaptic cleft refers to a microscopic gap between the terminal button of a neuron and the cell membrane of another neuron.
Conditional stimulus	A conditional stimulus in a conditional reflex elicits a conditional response.
Prefrontal cortex	The prefrontal cortex is the anterior part of the frontal lobes of the brain, lying in front of the motor and associative areas. It has been implicated in planning complex cognitive behaviors, personality expression and moderating correct social behavior. The prefrontal cortex continues to develop until around age 6.

Projection	Attributing one's own undesirable thoughts, impulses, traits, or behaviors to others is referred to as projection.
Glutamate	Glutamate is one of the 20 standard amino acids used by all organisms in their proteins. It is critical for proper cell function, but it is not an essential nutrient in humans because it can be manufactured from other compounds.
Sigmund Freud	Sigmund Freud was the founder of the psychoanalytic school, based on his theory that unconscious motives control much behavior, that particular kinds of unconscious thoughts and memories are the source of neurosis, and that neurosis could be treated through bringing these unconscious thoughts and memories to consciousness in psychoanalytic treatment.
Neuroscience	A field that combines the work of psychologists, biologists, biochemists, medical researchers, and others in the study of the structure and function of the nervous system is neuroscience.
Lateralization	Lateralization refers to the dominance of one hemisphere of the brain for specific functions.
Forebrain	The forebrain is the highest level of the brain. Key structures in the forebrain are the limbic system, thalamus, basal ganglia, hypothalamus, and cerebral cortex.
Dyslexia	Dyslexia is a neurological disorder with biochemical and genetic markers. In its most common and apparent form, it is a disability in which a person's reading and/or writing ability is significantly lower than that which would be predicted by his or her general level of intelligence.
Cerebral lateralization	Functional specialization of the two hemispheres of the brain is called cerebral lateralization.
Right hemisphere	The brain is divided into left and right cerebral hemispheres. The right hemisphere of the cortex controls the left side of the body.
Corpus callosum	The corpus callosum is the largest white matter structure in the brain. It consists of mostly of contralateral axon projections. The corpus callosum connects the left and right cerebral hemispheres. Most communication between regions in different halves of the brain are carried over the corpus callosum.

Brain	The brain controls and coordinates most movement, behavior and homeostatic body functions such as heartbeat, blood pressure, fluid balance and body temperature. Functions of the brain are responsible for cognition, emotion, memory, motor learning and other sorts of learning. The brain is primarily made up of two types of cells: glia and neurons.
Cerebral hemisphere	Either of the two halves that make up the cerebrum is referred to as a cerebral hemisphere. The hemispheres operate together, linked by the corpus callosum, a very large bundle of nerve fibers, and also by other smaller commissures.
Forebrain	The forebrain is the highest level of the brain. Key structures in the forebrain are the limbic system, thalamus, basal ganglia, hypothalamus, and cerebral cortex.
Right hemisphere	The brain is divided into left and right cerebral hemispheres. The right hemisphere of the cortex controls the left side of the body.
Left hemisphere	The left hemisphere of the cortex controls the right side of the body, coordinates complex movements, and, in 95% of people, controls the production of speech and written language.
Society	The social sciences use the term society to mean a group of people that form a semi-closed (or semi-open) social system, in which most interactions are with other individuals belonging to the group.
Aphasia	Aphasia is a loss or impairment of the ability to produce or comprehend language, due to brain damage. It is usually a result of damage to the language centers of the brain.
Apraxia	Apraxia is a neurological disorder characterized by loss of the ability to execute or carry out learned movements, despite having the desire and the physical ability to perform the movements.
Motor cortex	Motor cortex refers to the section of cortex that lies in the frontal lobe, just across the central fissure from the sensory cortex. Neural impulses in the motor cortex are linked to muscular responses throughout the body.
Lesion	A lesion is a non-specific term referring to abnormal tissue in the body. It can be caused by any disease process including trauma (physical, chemical, electrical), infection, neoplasm, metabolic and autoimmune.
Prefrontal cortex	The prefrontal cortex is the anterior part of the frontal lobes of the brain, lying in front of the motor and associative areas. It has been implicated in planning complex cognitive behaviors, personality expression and moderating correct social behavior. The prefrontal cortex continues to develop until around age 6.
Lateralization	Lateralization refers to the dominance of one hemisphere of the brain for specific functions.
Cerebral lateralization	Functional specialization of the two hemispheres of the brain is called cerebral lateralization.
Brain imaging	Brain imaging is a fairly recent discipline within medicine and neuroscience. Brain imaging falls into two broad categories -- structural imaging and functional imaging.
Dichotic listening	Dichotic Listening is a procedure used for investigating selective attention in the auditory domain. Two messages are presented to both the left and right ears, normally using a set of headphones. Normally, participants are asked to pay attention to either one, or both of the messages and may later be asked about the content of both.
Mutism	Mutism refers to refusal or inability to talk.
Handedness	A preference for the right or left hand in most activities is referred to as handedness. Right-handedness is dominant in all cultures, and it appears before culture can influence the child.

Functional magnetic resonance imaging	Functional Magnetic Resonance Imaging describes the use of MRI to measure hemodynamic signals related to neural activity in the brain or spinal cord of humans or other animals. It is one of the most recently developed forms of brain imaging.
Magnetic resonance imaging	Magnetic resonance imaging is a method of creating images of the inside of opaque organs in living organisms as well as detecting the amount of bound water in geological structures. It is primarily used to demonstrate pathological or other physiological alterations of living tissues and is a commonly used form of medical imaging.
Penfield	Penfield treated patients with severe epilepsy by destroying nerve cells in the brain. Before operating, he stimulated the brain with electrical probes while the patients were conscious on the operating table, and observed their responses. It allowed him to create maps of sensory and motor functions.
Population	Population refers to all members of a well-defined group of organisms, events, or things.
Stroke	A stroke occurs when the blood supply to a part of the brain is suddenly interrupted by occlusion, by hemorrhage, or other causes
Hypothesis	A specific statement about behavior or mental processes that is testable through research is a hypothesis.
Corpus callosum	The corpus callosum is the largest white matter structure in the brain. It consists of mostly of contralateral axon projections. The corpus callosum connects the left and right cerebral hemispheres. Most communication between regions in different halves of the brain are carried over the corpus callosum.
Axon	An axon, or "nerve fiber," is a long slender projection of a nerve cell, or "neuron," which conducts electrical impulses away from the neuron's cell body or soma.
Species	Species refers to a reproductively isolated breeding population.
Sperry	Sperry separated the corpus callosum, the area of the brain used to transfer signals between the right and left hemispheres, to treat epileptics. He then tested these patients with tasks that were known to be dependant on specific hemispheres of the brain and demonstrated that the two halves of the brain now had independent functions.
Discrimination	In Learning theory, discrimination refers the ability to distinguish between a conditioned stimulus and other stimuli. It can be brought about by extensive training or differential reinforcement. In social terms, it is the denial of privileges to a person or a group on the basis of prejudice.
Optic chiasm	Optic chiasm refers to the point at which the optic nerves from the inside half of each eye cross over and then project to the opposite half of the brain.
Experimental group	Experimental group refers to any group receiving a treatment effect in an experiment.
Control group	A group that does not receive the treatment effect in an experiment is referred to as the control group or sometimes as the comparison group.
Scotoma	The Scotoma is an area of loss of visual acuity surrounded by a field of normal or relatively well-preserved vision. Every normal eye has a scotoma in its field of vision, usually termed its blind spot. Others may occur from damage.
Retina	The retina is a thin layer of cells at the back of the eyeball. It is the part of the eye which converts light into nervous signals. The retina contains photoreceptor cells which receive the light; the resulting neural signals then undergo complex processing by other neurons of the retina, and are transformed into action potentials in retinal ganglion cells

	whose axons form the optic nerve.
Baseline	Measure of a particular behavior or process taken before the introduction of the independent variable or treatment is called the baseline.
Somatosensory	Somatosensory system consists of the various sensory receptors that trigger the experiences labelled as touch or pressure, temperature, pain, and the sensations of muscle movement and joint position including posture, movement, and facial expression.
Gazzaniga	Gazzaniga worked under the guidance of Roger Sperry, with primary responsibility for initiating human split-brain research. In his subsequent work he has made important advances in our understanding of functional lateralization in the brain and how the cerebral hemispheres communicate with one another.
Tactile	Pertaining to the sense of touch is referred to as tactile.
Consciousness	The awareness of the sensations, thoughts, and feelings being experienced at a given moment is called consciousness.
Emotion	An emotion is a mental states that arise spontaneously, rather than through conscious effort. They are often accompanied by physiological changes.
Stream of consciousness	James' concept that the mind is a continuous flow of sensations, images, thoughts, and feelings is stream of consciousness. Accordingly, consiousness cannot be reduced into elements.
Stimulus	A change in an environmental condition that elicits a response is a stimulus.
Seizure	A seizure is a temporary alteration in brain function expressed as a changed mental state, tonic or clonic movements and various other symptoms. They are due to temporary abnormal electrical activity of a group of brain cells.
Perception	Perception is the process of acquiring, interpreting, selecting, and organizing sensory information.
Control subjects	Control subjects are participants in an experiment who do not receive the treatment effect but for whom all other conditions are held comparable to those of experimental subjects.
Theories	Theories are logically self-consistent models or frameworks describing the behavior of a certain natural or social phenomenon. They are broad explanations and predictions concerning phenomena of interest.
Gyrus	A gyrus is a ridge on the cerebral cortex. It is generally surrounded by one or more sulci.
Planum temporale	The planum temporale is the posterior superior surface of the superior temporal gyrus in the cerebrum. It is a highly lateralized brain structure involved with language.
Lateral fissure	The lateral fissure is one of the most prominent structures of the human brain. It divides the frontal lobe and parietal lobe above from the temporal lobe below.
Temporal lobe	The temporal lobe is part of the cerebrum. It lies at the side of the brain, beneath the lateral or Sylvian fissure. Adjacent areas in the superior, posterior and lateral parts of the temporal lobe are involved in high-level auditory processing.
Primary auditory cortex	The primary auditory cortex is responsible for processing of auditory information. It is located in the temporal lobe; the posterior half of the superior temporal gyrus and also dives into the lateral sulcus as the transverse temporal gyri.
Cerebral cortex	The cerebral cortex is the outermost layer of the cerebrum and has a grey color. It is made up of four lobes and it is involved in many complex brain functions including memory, perceptual awareness, "thinking", language and consciousness. The cerebral cortex receives sensory information from many different sensory organs eg: eyes, ears, etc. and processes the

	information.
Frontal lobe	The frontal lobe comprises four major folds of cortical tissue: the precentral gyrus, superior gyrus and the middle gyrus of the frontal gyri, the inferior frontal gyrus. It has been found to play a part in impulse control, judgement, language, memory, motor function, problem solving, sexual behavior, socialization and spontaneity.
Neuroanatomy	Neuroanatomy is the study of the anatomy of the central nervous system.
Pitch	Pitch is the psychological interpretation of a sound or musical tone corresponding to its physical frequency
Adaptation	Adaptation is a lowering of sensitivity to a stimulus following prolonged exposure to that stimulus. Behavioral adaptations are special ways a particular organism behaves to survive in its natural habitat.
Premise	A premise is a statement presumed true within the context of a discourse, especially of a logical argument.
Evolution	Commonly used to refer to gradual change, evolution is the change in the frequency of alleles within a population from one generation to the next. This change may be caused by different mechanisms, including natural selection, genetic drift, or changes in population (gene flow).
Empirical	Empirical means the use of working hypotheses which are capable of being disproved using observation or experiment.
American Sign Language	The American Sign Language is a language of hand gestures used by deaf and hearing impaired persons.
Neuropsychologist	A psychologist concerned with the relationships among cognition, affect, behavior, and brain function is a neuropsychologist.
Dissociation	Dissociation is a psychological state or condition in which certain thoughts, emotions, sensations, or memories are separated from the rest.
Antecedents	In behavior modification, events that typically precede the target response are called antecedents.
Carl Wernicke	Carl Wernicke discovered the left cerebral hemisphere's speech centre.
Syndrome	The term syndrome is the association of several clinically recognizable features, signs, symptoms, phenomena or characteristics which often occur together, so that the presence of one feature indicates the presence of the others.
Intonation	The use of pitches of varying levels to help communicate meaning is called intonation.
Visual cortex	The visual cortex is the general term applied to both the primary visual cortex and the visual association area. Anatomically, the visual cortex occupies the entire occipital lobe, the inferior temporal lobe (IT), posterior parts of the parietal lobe, and a few small regions in the frontal lobe.
Neuron	The neuron is the primary cell of the nervous system. They are found in the brain, the spinal cord, in the nerves and ganglia of the peripheral nervous system. It is a specialized cell that conducts impulses through the nervous system and contains three major parts: cell body, dendrites, and an axon. It can have many dendrites but only one axon.
Validity	The extent to which a test measures what it is intended to measure is called validity.
Empirical evidence	Facts or information based on direct observation or experience are referred to as empirical evidence.
Case study	A carefully drawn biography that may be obtained through interviews, questionnaires, and

	psychological tests is called a case study.
Tumor	A tumor is an abnormal growth that when located in the brain can either be malignant and directly destroy brain tissue, or be benign and disrupt functioning by increasing intracranial pressure.
Stages	Stages represent relatively discrete periods of time in which functioning is qualitatively different from functioning at other periods.
Lobes	The four major sections of the cerebral cortex: frontal, parietal, temporal, and occipital are called lobes.
White matter	White matter is one of the two main solid components of the central nervous system. It is composed of axons which connect various grey matter areas of the brain to each other and carry nerve impulses between neurons.
Cingulate cortex	The part of the limbic system that is believed to process cognitive information in emotion is the cingulate cortex. The cingulate cortex is part of the brain and situated roughly in the middle of the cortex.
Local anesthetic	Local anesthetic drugs act mainly by inhibiting sodium influx through sodium-specific ion channels in the neuronal cell membrane, in particular the so-called voltage-gated sodium channels. When the influx of sodium is interrupted, an action potential cannot arise and signal conduction is thus inhibited.
Electrode	Any device used to electrically stimulate nerve tissue or to record its activity is an electrode.
Somatosensory cortex	The primary somatosensory cortex is across the central sulcus and behind the primary motor cortex configured to generally correspond with the arrangement of nearby motor cells related to specific body parts. It is the main sensory receptive area for the sense of touch.
Phoneme	In oral language, a phoneme is the theoretical basic unit of sound that can be used to distinguish words or morphemes; in sign language, it is a similarly basic unit of hand shape, motion, position, or facial expression.
Neuroscience	A field that combines the work of psychologists, biologists, biochemists, medical researchers, and others in the study of the structure and function of the nervous system is neuroscience.
Homogeneous	In biology homogeneous has a meaning similar to its meaning in mathematics. Generally it means "the same" or "of the same quality or general property".
Dyslexia	Dyslexia is a neurological disorder with biochemical and genetic markers. In its most common and apparent form, it is a disability in which a person's reading and/or writing ability is significantly lower than that which would be predicted by his or her general level of intelligence.
Learning	Learning is a relatively permanent change in behavior that results from experience. Thus, to attribute a behavioral change to learning, the change must be relatively permanent and must result from experience.
Heritability	Heritability It is that proportion of the observed variation in a particular phenotype within a particular population, that can be attributed to the contribution of genotype. In other words: it measures the extent to which differences between individuals in a population are due their being different genetically.
Fisher	Fisher was a eugenicist, evolutionary biologist, geneticist and statistician. He has been described as "The greatest of Darwin's successors", and a genius who almost single-handedly created the foundations for modern statistical science inventing the techniques of maximum

likelihood and analysis of variance.

Cultural diversity Cultural diversity is the variety of human societies or cultures in a specific region, or in the world as a whole.

Occipital lobe The occipital lobe is the smallest of four true lobes in the human brain. Located in the rearmost portion of the skull, the occipital lobe is part of the forebrain structure. It is the visual processing center.

Wisdom Wisdom is the ability to make correct judgments and decisions. It is an intangible quality gained through experience. Whether or not something is wise is determined in a pragmatic sense by its popularity, how long it has been around, and its ability to predict against future events.

Lobotomy A lobotomy is the intentional severing of the prefrontal cortex from the thalamic region of the brain. The frontal lobe of the brain controls a number of advanced cognitive functions, as well as motor control. Today, lobotomy is very infrequently practised. It may be a treatment of last resort for obsessive-compulsive sufferers, and may also be used for people suffering chronic pain.

Biopsychology	Biopsychology is the scientific study of the biological bases of behavior and mental states. Empirical experiments study changes in central nervous system activation in response to a stimulus.
Emotion	An emotion is a mental states that arise spontaneously, rather than through conscious effort. They are often accompanied by physiological changes.
Chronic	Chronic refers to a relatively long duration, usually more than a few months.
Biopsychologist	A psychologist who studies the relationship between behavior and biological processes, especially activity in the nervous system is referred to as a Biopsychologist.
Launching	The process in which youths move into adulthood and exit their family of origin is called launching. It can be a time to formulate life goals, to develop an identity, and to become more independent before joining with another person to form a new family.
Brain	The brain controls and coordinates most movement, behavior and homeostatic body functions such as heartbeat, blood pressure, fluid balance and body temperature. Functions of the brain are responsible for cognition, emotion, memory, motor learning and other sorts of learning. The brain is primarily made up of two types of cells: glia and neurons.
Personality	Personality refers to the pattern of enduring characteristics that differentiates a person, the patterns of behaviors that make each individual unique.
Neurologist	A physician who studies the nervous system, especially its structure, functions, and abnormalities is referred to as neurologist.
Harlow	Harlow and his famous wire and cloth surrogate mother monkey studies demonstrated that the need for affection created a stronger bond between mother and infant than did physical needs. He also found that the more discrimination problems the monkeys solved, the better they became at solving them.
Lobes	The four major sections of the cerebral cortex: frontal, parietal, temporal, and occipital are called lobes.
Evolution	Commonly used to refer to gradual change, evolution is the change in the frequency of alleles within a population from one generation to the next. This change may be caused by different mechanisms, including natural selection, genetic drift, or changes in population (gene flow).
Darwin	Darwin achieved lasting fame as originator of the theory of evolution through natural selection. His book Expression of Emotions in Man and Animals is generally considered the first text on comparative psychology.
Species	Species refers to a reproductively isolated breeding population.
Anecdotal evidence	Anecdotal evidence is unreliable evidence based on personal experience that has not been empirically tested, and which is often used in an argument as if it had been scientifically or statistically proven. The person using anecdotal evidence may or may not be aware of the fact that, by doing so, they are generalizing.
Phineas Gage	As a result of an injury to his brain, Phineas Gage reportedly had significant changes in personality and temperament, which provided some of the first evidence that specific parts of the brain, particularly the frontal lobes, might be involved in specific psychological processes dealing with emotion, personality and problem solving.
Stages	Stages represent relatively discrete periods of time in which functioning is qualitatively different from functioning at other periods.
Skeletal muscle	Skeletal muscle is a type of striated muscle, attached to the skeleton. They are used to facilitate movement, by applying force to bones and joints; via contraction. They generally contract voluntarily (via nerve stimulation), although they can contract involuntarily.

Nervous system The body's electrochemical communication circuitry, made up of billions of neurons is a nervous system.

Theories Theories are logically self-consistent models or frameworks describing the behavior of a certain natural or social phenomenon. They are broad explanations and predictions concerning phenomena of interest.

Lange Lange along with William James, independently developed the James-Lange theory of emotion. Unlike James, Lange specifically stated that vasomotor changes are emotions. Lange also noted the psychotropic effects of lithium, although his work in this area was forgotten and independently rediscovered much later.

Autonomic nervous system A division of the peripheral nervous system, the autonomic nervous system, regulates glands and activities such as heartbeat, respiration, digestion, and dilation of the pupils. It is responsible for homeostasis, maintaining a relatively constant internal environment .

Somatic nervous system The somatic nervous system is the part of the peripheral nervous system associated with the voluntary control of body movements through the action of skeletal muscles. The somatic nervous system consists of afferent fibers which receive information from external sources, and efferent fibers which are responsible for muscle contraction.

Feedback Feedback refers to information returned to a person about the effects a response has had.

Perception Perception is the process of acquiring, interpreting, selecting, and organizing sensory information.

Stimulus A change in an environmental condition that elicits a response is a stimulus.

Hypothalamus The hypothalamus is a region of the brain located below the thalamus, forming the major portion of the ventral region of the diencephalon and functioning to regulate certain metabolic processes and other autonomic activities.

Cerebral hemisphere Either of the two halves that make up the cerebrum is referred to as a cerebral hemisphere. The hemispheres operate together, linked by the corpus callosum, a very large bundle of nerve fibers, and also by other smaller commissures.

Limbic system The limbic system is a group of brain structures that are involved in various emotions such as aggression, fear, pleasure and also in the formation of memory. The limbic system affects the endocrine system and the autonomic nervous system. It consists of several subcortical structures located around the thalamus.

Temporal lobe The temporal lobe is part of the cerebrum. It lies at the side of the brain, beneath the lateral or Sylvian fissure. Adjacent areas in the superior, posterior and lateral parts of the temporal lobe are involved in high-level auditory processing.

Syndrome The term syndrome is the association of several clinically recognizable features, signs, symptoms, phenomena or characteristics which often occur together, so that the presence of one feature indicates the presence of the others.

Amygdala Located in the brain's medial temporal lobe, the almond-shaped amygdala is believed to play a key role in the emotions. It forms part of the limbic system and is linked to both fear responses and pleasure. Its size is positively correlated with aggressive behavior across species.

Thalamus An area near the center of the brain involved in the relay of sensory information to the cortex and in the functions of sleep and attention is the thalamus.

Epinephrine Epinephrine is a hormone and a neurotransmitter. Epinephrine plays a central role in the short-term stress reaction—the physiological response to threatening or exciting conditions. It is secreted by the adrenal medulla. When released into the bloodstream, epinephrine binds

	to multiple receptors and has numerous effects throughout the body.
Norepinephrine	Norepinephrine is released from the adrenal glands as a hormone into the blood, but it is also a neurotransmitter in the nervous system. As a stress hormone, it affects parts of the human brain where attention and impulsivity are controlled. Along with epinephrine, this compound effects the fight-or-flight response, activating the sympathetic nervous system to directly increase heart rate, release energy from fat, and increase muscle readiness.
Sympathetic	The sympathetic nervous system activates what is often termed the "fight or flight response". It is an automatic regulation system, that is, one that operates without the intervention of conscious thought.
Pupil	In the eye, the pupil is the opening in the middle of the iris. It appears black because most of the light entering it is absorbed by the tissues inside the eye. The size of the pupil is controlled by involuntary contraction and dilation of the iris, in order to regulate the intensity of light entering the eye. This is known as the pupillary reflex.
Adrenal medulla	Composed mainly of hormone-producing chromaffin cells, the adrenal medulla is the principal site of the conversion of the amino acid tyrosine into the catecholamines epinephrine and norepinephrine (also called adrenaline and noradrenaline, respectively).
Polygraph	A polygraph is a device which measures and records several physiological variables such as blood pressure, heart rate, respiration and skin conductivity while a series of questions is being asked, in an attempt to detect lies.
Guilt	Guilt describes many concepts related to a negative emotion or condition caused by actions which are believed to be, morally wrong. According to Freud, the avoidance of guilt is the basis for moral behavior.
Ekman	Ekman found that at least some facial expressions and their corresponding emotions are not culturally determined, and thus presumably biological in origin. Expressions he found to be universal included anger, disgust, fear, joy, sadness and surprise.
Variable	A variable refers to a measurable factor, characteristic, or attribute of an individual or a system.
Hypothesis	A specific statement about behavior or mental processes that is testable through research is a hypothesis.
Zajonc	Zajonc is best known for his decades of work on the mere exposure effect, the phenomenon that repeated exposure to a stimulus brings about an attitude change in relation to the stimulus.
Facial feedback hypothesis	The facial feedback hypothesis states that facial expressions can influence emotions, as well as reflect them.
Affect	A subjective feeling or emotional tone often accompanied by bodily expressions noticeable to others is called affect.
Insight	Insight refers to a sudden awareness of the relationships among various elements that had previously appeared to be independent of one another.
Testosterone	Testosterone is a steroid hormone from the androgen group. It is the principal male sex hormone and the "original" anabolic steroid.
Castration	Castration is any action, surgical, chemical or otherwise, by which a biological male loses use of the testes. This causes sterilization, i.e. prevents him from reproducing; it also greatly reduces the production of certain hormones, such as testosterone.
Puberty	Puberty refers to the process of physical changes by which a child's body becomes an adult body capable of reproduction.

Selye	Selye did much important theoretical work on the non-specific response of the organism to stress. Selye discovered and documented that stress differs from other physical responses in that stress is stressful whether the one receives good or bad news, whether the impulse is positive or negative. He called negative stress distress and positive stress eustress.
Physiological changes	Alterations in heart rate, blood pressure, perspiration, and other involuntary responses are physiological changes.
Life span	Life span refers to the upper boundary of life, the maximum number of years an individual can live. The maximum life span of human beings is about 120 years of age. Females live an average of 6 years longer than males.
Testes	Testes are the male reproductive glands or gonads; this is where sperm develop and are stored.
Lesion	A lesion is a non-specific term referring to abnormal tissue in the body. It can be caused by any disease process including trauma (physical, chemical, electrical), infection, neoplasm, metabolic and autoimmune.
Adrenal cortex	Adrenal cortex refers to the outer layer of the adrenal glands, which produces hormones that affect salt intake, reactions to stress, and sexual development.
Control subjects	Control subjects are participants in an experiment who do not receive the treatment effect but for whom all other conditions are held comparable to those of experimental subjects.
Immune system	The most important function of the human immune system occurs at the cellular level of the blood and tissues. The lymphatic and blood circulation systems are highways for specialized white blood cells. These cells include B cells, T cells, natural killer cells, and macrophages. All function with the primary objective of recognizing, attacking and destroying bacteria, viruses, cancer cells, and all substances seen as foreign.
Psychoneuroimunology	Psychoneuroimmunology is a specialist field of research that studies the connection between the brain, or mental states, and the immunal and hormonal systems of the human body.
Lymphocyte	A lymphocyte is a type of white blood cell involved in the human body's immune system. There are two broad categories, namely T cells and B cells. The lymphocyte play an important and integral part of the body's defenses.
Macrophage	Macrophage refers to the cells found in tissues that are responsible for phagocytosis of pathogens, dead cells and cellular debris. They are part of the innate immune system.
Antibody	An antibody is a protein used by the immune system to identify and neutralize foreign objects like bacteria and viruses. Each antibody recognizes a specific antigen unique to its target.
T cells	T cells are a subset of lymphocytes that play a large role in the immune response. Some attack antigens directly while others help regulate the system.
B cells	B cells are lymphocytes that play a large role in the humoral immune response.
Antigen	An antigen is a molecule that stimulates the production of antibodies. Usually, it is a protein or a polysaccharide, but can be any type of molecule, including small molecules (haptens) coupled to a protein (carrier).
Receptor	A sensory receptor is a structure that recognizes a stimulus in the internal or external environment of an organism. In response to stimuli the sensory receptor initiates sensory transduction by creating graded potentials or action potentials in the same cell or in an adjacent one.
Empirical	Empirical means the use of working hypotheses which are capable of being disproved using observation or experiment.

Empirical evidence	Facts or information based on direct observation or experience are referred to as empirical evidence.
Evolutionary psychology	Evolutionary psychology proposes that cognition and behavior can be better understood in light of evolutionary history.
Maladaptive	In psychology, a behavior or trait is adaptive when it helps an individual adjust and function well within their social environment. A maladaptive behavior or trait is counterproductive to the individual.
Acute	Acute means sudden, sharp, and abrupt. Usually short in duration.
Neuropeptides	Brain chemicals, such as enkephalins and endorphins, that regulate the activity of neurons are called neuropeptides.
Neuron	The neuron is the primary cell of the nervous system. They are found in the brain, the spinal cord, in the nerves and ganglia of the peripheral nervous system. It is a specialized cell that conducts impulses through the nervous system and contains three major parts: cell body, dendrites, and an axon. It can have many dendrites but only one axon.
Correlational study	A correlational study observes or measures two or more variables to find relationships between them. Such studies can identify lawful relationships but cannot determine whether change in one variable is the cause of change in another.
Correlation	A statistical technique for determining the degree of association between two or more variables is referred to as correlation.
Positive correlation	A relationship between two variables in which both vary in the same direction is called a positive correlation.
Prenatal	Prenatal period refers to the time from conception to birth.
Infancy	The developmental period that extends from birth to 18 or 24 months is called infancy.
Hippocampus	The hippocampus is a part of the brain located inside the temporal lobe. It forms a part of the limbic system and plays a part in memory and navigation.
Neurogenesis	Neurogenesis literally means "birth of neurons". Neurogenesis is most prevalent during prenatal development and is the process by which neurons are created to populate the growing brain.
Population	Population refers to all members of a well-defined group of organisms, events, or things.
Subjective experience	Subjective experience refers to reality as it is perceived and interpreted, not as it exists objectively.
Estradiol	Estradiol is a sex hormone. Labelled the "female" hormone but also present in males it represents the major estrogen in humans. Critical for sexual functioning estradiol also supports bone growth.
Conditioning	Conditioning describes the process by which behaviors can be learned or modified through interaction with the environment.
Nucleus	In neuroanatomy, a cluster of cell bodies of neurons within the central nervous system is a nucleus.
Conditional stimulus	A conditional stimulus in a conditional reflex elicits a conditional response.
Anatomy	Anatomy is the branch of biology that deals with the structure and organization of living things. It can be divided into animal anatomy (zootomy) and plant anatomy (phytonomy). Major branches of anatomy include comparative anatomy, histology, and human anatomy.

Fear response	In the Mowrer-Miller theory, a response to a threatening or noxious situation that is covert but that is assumed to function as a stimulus to produce measurable physiological changes in the body and observable overt behavior is referred to as the fear response.
Premise	A premise is a statement presumed true within the context of a discourse, especially of a logical argument.
Prefrontal cortex	The prefrontal cortex is the anterior part of the frontal lobes of the brain, lying in front of the motor and associative areas. It has been implicated in planning complex cognitive behaviors, personality expression and moderating correct social behavior. The prefrontal cortex continues to develop until around age 6.
Epilepsy	Epilepsy is a chronic neurological condition characterized by recurrent unprovoked neural discharges. It is commonly controlled with medication, although surgical methods are used as well.
Genetic disorder	A genetic disorder is a disease caused by abnormal expression of one or more genes in a person causing a clinical phenotype.
Learning	Learning is a relatively permanent change in behavior that results from experience. Thus, to attribute a behavioral change to learning, the change must be relatively permanent and must result from experience.
Lateralization	Lateralization refers to the dominance of one hemisphere of the brain for specific functions.
Brain imaging	Brain imaging is a fairly recent discipline within medicine and neuroscience. Brain imaging falls into two broad categories -- structural imaging and functional imaging.
Cerebral lateralization	Functional specialization of the two hemispheres of the brain is called cerebral lateralization.
Right hemisphere	The brain is divided into left and right cerebral hemispheres. The right hemisphere of the cortex controls the left side of the body.
Left hemisphere	The left hemisphere of the cortex controls the right side of the body, coordinates complex movements, and, in 95% of people, controls the production of speech and written language.
Prosody	Prosody consists of the distinctive variations of stress, tone, and timing in spoken language. How pitch changes from word to word, the speed of speech, the loudness of speech, and the duration of pauses all contribute to prosody.
Extraversion	Extraversion, one of the big-five personailty traits, is marked by pronounced engagement with the external world. They are people who enjoy being with people, are full of energy, and often experience positive emotions.
Neuroticism	Eysenck's use of the term neuroticism (or Emotional Stability) was proposed as the dimension describing individual differences in the predisposition towards neurotic disorder.
Evolutionary perspective	A perspective that focuses on how humans have evolved and adapted behaviors required for survival against various environmental pressures over the long course is called the evolutionary perspective.
Comparative research	Comparative research is a research methodology that aims to make comparisons across different countries or cultures. A major problem is that the data sets in different countries may not use the same categories, or define categories differently.
Neuroscience	A field that combines the work of psychologists, biologists, biochemists, medical researchers, and others in the study of the structure and function of the nervous system is neuroscience.
Gene	A gene is an ultramicroscopic area of the chromosome. It is the smallest physical unit of the

DNA molecule that carries a piece of hereditary information.

Psychiatrist	A psychiatrist is a physician who specializes in the diagnosis and treatment of psychological disorders.
Psychological disorder	Mental processes and/or behavior patterns that cause emotional distress and/or substantial impairment in functioning is a psychological disorder.
Clinical psychologist	A psychologist, usually with a Ph.D, whose training is in the diagnosis, treatment, or research of psychological and behavioral disorders is a clinical psychologist.
Emotion	An emotion is a mental states that arise spontaneously, rather than through conscious effort. They are often accompanied by physiological changes.
Schizophrenia	Schizophrenia is characterized by persistent defects in the perception or expression of reality. A person suffering from untreated schizophrenia typically demonstrates grossly disorganized thinking, and may also experience delusions or auditory hallucinations
Early adulthood	The developmental period beginning in the late teens or early twenties and lasting into the thirties is called early adulthood; characterized by an increasing self-awareness.
Adolescence	The period of life bounded by puberty and the assumption of adult responsibilities is adolescence.
Suicide	Suicide behavior is rare in childhood but escalates in adolescence. The suicide rate increases in a linear fashion from adolescence through late adulthood.
Hyperactivity	Hyperactivity can be described as a state in which a individual is abnormally easily excitable and exuberant. Strong emotional reactions and a very short span of attention is also typical for the individual.
Waxy flexibility	A feature of catatonic schizophrenia in which persons maintain postures into which they are placed is referred to as waxy flexibility.
Hallucination	A hallucination is a sensory perception experienced in the absence of an external stimulus, as distinct from an illusion, which is a misperception of an external stimulus. They may occur in any sensory modality - visual, auditory, olfactory, gustatory, tactile, or mixed.
Catatonia	Catatonia is a very severe psychiatric and medical condition, characterized by, in catatonic stupor, a general absence of motor activity, and, in catatonic excitement, violent, hyperactive behavior directed at oneself or others but with no visible purpose.
Echolalia	Echolalia is the repetition or echoing of verbal utterances made by another person. Up to 75% of autistics exhibit echolalia in some form, but it also affects the mentally retarded and schizophrenic to lesser degrees as well as catatonic depressed patients. It is also experienced by those with Tourette Syndrome.
Mental illness	Mental illness is the term formerly used to mean psychological disorder but less preferred because it implies that the causes of the disorder can be found in a medical disease process.
Identical twins	Identical twins occur when a single egg is fertilized to form one zygote (monozygotic) but the zygote then divides into two separate embryos. The two embryos develop into foetuses sharing the same womb. Monozygotic twins are genetically identical unless there has been a mutation in development, and they are almost always the same gender.
Chromosome	The DNA which carries genetic information in biological cells is normally packaged in the form of one or more large macromolecules called a chromosome. Humans normally have 46.
Cowan	Cowan regards working memory not as a separate system, but as a part of long-term memory. Representations in working memory are a subset of the representations in long-term memory.
Chlorpromazine	Chlorpromazine was the first antipsychotic drug, used during the 1950s and 1960s. Used as chlorpromazine hydrochloride and sold under the tradenames Largactil (the "liquid cosh") and

	Thorazine, it has sedative, hypotensive and antiemetic properties as well as anticholinergic and antidopaminergic effects. Today, Chlorpromazine is considered a typical antipsychotic.
Reserpine	Reserpine is an indole alkaloid antipsychotic and antihypertensive drug known to irreversibly bind to storage vesicles of neurotransmitters such as dopamine, norepinephrine, and serotonin. This leads to depletion of the neurotransmitters and subsequent depression in humans.
Dopamine	Dopamine is critical to the way the brain controls our movements and is a crucial part of the basal ganglia motor loop. It is commonly associated with the 'pleasure system' of the brain, providing feelings of enjoyment and reinforcement to motivate us to do, or continue doing, certain activities.
Metabolites	Metabolites are the intermediates and products of metabolism.
Evolution	Commonly used to refer to gradual change, evolution is the change in the frequency of alleles within a population from one generation to the next. This change may be caused by different mechanisms, including natural selection, genetic drift, or changes in population (gene flow).
Brain	The brain controls and coordinates most movement, behavior and homeostatic body functions such as heartbeat, blood pressure, fluid balance and body temperature. Functions of the brain are responsible for cognition, emotion, memory, motor learning and other sorts of learning. The brain is primarily made up of two types of cells: glia and neurons.
Receptor	A sensory receptor is a structure that recognizes a stimulus in the internal or external environment of an organism. In response to stimuli the sensory receptor initiates sensory transduction by creating graded potentials or action potentials in the same cell or in an adjacent one.
Synapse	A synapse is specialized junction through which cells of the nervous system signal to one another and to non-neuronal cells such as muscles or glands.
Feedback	Feedback refers to information returned to a person about the effects a response has had.
Psychopharma-ology	Psychopharmacology refers to the study of the effects of drugs on the mind and on behavior; also known as medication and drug therapy.
Neuron	The neuron is the primary cell of the nervous system. They are found in the brain, the spinal cord, in the nerves and ganglia of the peripheral nervous system. It is a specialized cell that conducts impulses through the nervous system and contains three major parts: cell body, dendrites, and an axon. It can have many dendrites but only one axon.
Haloperidol	Haloperidol is a conventional butyrophenone antipsychotic drug. It posesses a strong activity against delusions and hallucinations, most likely due to an effective dopaminergic receptor blockage in the mesocortex and the limbic system of the brain.
Phenothiazine	Phenothiazines are the largest of the 5 main classes of antipsychotic drugs. Although these drugs are generally effective, there are often serious side-effects including Parkinsonism and sedation (especially in the early stages of treatment).
Neuroleptics	Neuroleptics are a group of drugs used to treat psychosis. Common conditions with which neuroleptics might be used include schizophrenia, mania and delusional disorder. They also have some effects as mood stabilizers, leading to their frequent use in treating mood disorder (particularly bipolar disorder) even when no signs of psychosis are present.
Correlation	A statistical technique for determining the degree of association between two or more variables is referred to as correlation.
Positive correlation	A relationship between two variables in which both vary in the same direction is called a positive correlation.

Glutamate	Glutamate is one of the 20 standard amino acids used by all organisms in their proteins. It is critical for proper cell function, but it is not an essential nutrient in humans because it can be manufactured from other compounds.
Neurotransmitter	A neurotransmitter is a chemical that is used to relay, amplify and modulate electrical signals between a neurons and another cell.
Clozapine	Clozapine (trade names Clozaril), was the first of the atypical antipsychotic drugs. Clozapine is the only FDA-approved medication indicated for treatment-resistant schizophrenia and for reducing the risk of suicidal behavior in patients with schizophrenia.
Serotonin	Serotonin, a neurotransmitter, is believed to play an important part of the biochemistry of depression, bipolar disorder and anxiety. It is also believed to be influential on sexuality and appetite.
Blocking	If the one of the two members of a compound stimulus fails to produce the CR due to an earlier conditioning of the other member of the compound stimulus, blocking has occurred.
Depolarization	Depolarization is any change that decreases the absolute value of a cell's membrane potential. Thus, changes in membrane voltage in which the membrane potential becomes less positive or less negative are both depolarizations.
Cerebral cortex	The cerebral cortex is the outermost layer of the cerebrum and has a grey color. It is made up of four lobes and it is involved in many complex brain functions including memory, perceptual awareness, "thinking", language and consciousness. The cerebral cortex receives sensory information from many different sensory organs eg: eyes, ears, etc. and processes the information.
Pathology	Pathology is the study of the processes underlying disease and other forms of illness, harmful abnormality, or dysfunction.
Delusion	A false belief, not generally shared by others, and that cannot be changed despite strong evidence to the contrary is a delusion.
Affect	A subjective feeling or emotional tone often accompanied by bodily expressions noticeable to others is called affect.
Poverty of speech	Poverty of speech is a general lack of additional, unprompted content seen in normal speech. As a symptom, it is commonly seen in patients suffering from Schizophrenia. It can complicate psychotherapy severely because of the considerable difficulty in holding a fluent conversation.
Depression	In everyday language depression refers to any downturn in mood, which may be relatively transitory and perhaps due to something trivial. This is differentiated from Clinical depression which is marked by symptoms that last two weeks or more and are so severe that they interfere with daily living.
Clinical depression	Although nearly any mood with some element of sadness may colloquially be termed a depression, clinical depression is more than just a temporary state of sadness. Symptoms lasting two weeks or longer in duration, and of a severity that they begin to interfere with daily living.
Affective	Affective is the way people react emotionally, their ability to feel another living thing's pain or joy.
Mania	Mania is a medical condition characterized by severely elevated mood. Mania is most usually associated with bipolar disorder, where episodes of mania may cyclically alternate with episodes of depression.
Society	The social sciences use the term society to mean a group of people that form a semi-closed

	(or semi-open) social system, in which most interactions are with other individuals belonging to the group.
Bipolar Affective Disorder	Bipolar Affective Disorder is a mood disorder typically characterized by fluctuations between manic and depressive states; and, more generally, atypical mood regulation and mood instability.
Concordance	Concordance as used in genetics means the presence of the same trait in both members of a pair of twins, or in sets of individuals. A twin study examines the concordance rates of twins having the same trait, especially a disease, which can help determine how much the disease is affected by genetics versus environment.
Bipolar disorder	Bipolar Disorder is a mood disorder typically characterized by fluctuations between manic and depressive states; and, more generally, atypical mood regulation and mood instability.
Etiology	Etiology is the study of causation. The term is used in philosophy, physics and biology in reference to the causes of various phenomena. It is generally the study of why things occur, or even the reasons behind the way that things act.
Antidepressant	An antidepressant is a medication used primarily in the treatment of clinical depression. They are not thought to produce tolerance, although sudden withdrawal may produce adverse effects. They create little if any immediate change in mood and require between several days and several weeks to take effect.
Tricyclic	Tricyclic antidepressants are a class of antidepressant drugs first used in the 1950s. They are named after the drugs' molecular structure, which contains three rings of atoms.
Lithium	Lithium salts are used as mood stabilizing drugs primarily in the treatment of bipolar disorder, depression, and mania; but also in treating schizophrenia. Lithium is widely distributed in the central nervous system and interacts with a number of neurotransmitters and receptors, decreasing noradrenaline release and increasing serotonin synthesis.
Monoamine oxidase inhibitors	Monoamine oxidase inhibitors are a group of antidepressant drugs that prevent the enzyme monoamine oxidase from deactivating neurotransmitters of the central nervous system.
Tricyclic antidepressant	A tricyclic antidepressant is of a class of antidepressant drugs first used in the 1950s. They are named after the drugs' molecular structure, which contains three rings of atoms.
Monoamine oxidase	Monoamine oxidase is an enzyme that catalyzes the oxidation of monoamines. They are found bound to the outer membrane of mitochondria in most cell types in the body. Because of the vital role that it play in the inactivation of neurotransmitters, dysfunction (too much/too little MAO activity) is thought to be responsible for a number of neurological disorders.
Antidepressants	Antidepressants are medications used primarily in the treatment of clinical depression. Antidepressants create little if any immediate change in mood and require between several days and several weeks to take effect.
Norepinephrine	Norepinephrine is released from the adrenal glands as a hormone into the blood, but it is also a neurotransmitter in the nervous system. As a stress hormone, it affects parts of the human brain where attention and impulsivity are controlled. Along with epinephrine, this compound effects the fight-or-flight response, activating the sympathetic nervous system to directly increase heart rate, release energy from fat, and increase muscle readiness.
Cytoplasm	Cytoplasm is the colloidal, semi-fluid matter contained within the cell's plasma membrane, in which organelles are suspended. In contrast to the protoplasm, the cytoplasm does not include the cell nucleus, the interior of which is made up of nucleoplasm.
Agonist	Agonist refers to a drug that mimics or increases a neurotransmitter's effects.

Enzyme	An enzyme is a protein that catalyzes, or speeds up, a chemical reaction. Enzymes are essential to sustain life because most chemical reactions in biological cells would occur too slowly, or would lead to different products, without enzymes.
MAO inhibitors	MAO inhibitors are one of the major classes of drug prescribed for the treatment of depression. Serotonin is mainly broken down by MAO-A, as is norepinephrine and epinephrine (adrenaline), while phenethylamine is broken down by MAO-B. Both forms break down dopamine.
Stroke	A stroke occurs when the blood supply to a part of the brain is suddenly interrupted by occlusion, by hemorrhage, or other causes
Liver	The liver plays a major role in metabolism and has a number of functions in the body including detoxification, glycogen storage and plasma protein synthesis. It also produces bile, which is important for digestion. The liver converts most carbohydrates, proteing, and fats into glucose.
Imipramine	Imipramine is the first antidepressant to be developed in the late 1950s. The drug became a prototypical drug for the development of the later released tricyclics. It is not as commonly used today but sometimes used to treat major depression as a second-line treatment.
Reuptake	Reuptake is the reabsorption of a neurotransmitter by the molecular transporter of a pre-synaptic neuron after it has performed its function of transmitting a neural impulse.
Ion	An ion is an atom or group of atoms with a net electric charge. The energy required to detach an electron in its lowest energy state from an atom or molecule of a gas with less net electric charge is called the ionization potential, or ionization energy.
Fluoxetine	Fluoxetine is an antidepressant drug used medically in the treatment of depression, obsessive-compulsive disorder, bulimia nervosa, premenstrual dysphoric disorder and panic disorder. It is sold under the brand names Prozac®, and others.
Psychotherapy	Psychotherapy is a set of techniques based on psychological principles intended to improve mental health, emotional or behavioral issues.
Clinical psychology	Clinical psychology is involved in the diagnosis, assessment, and treatment of patients with mental or behavioral disorders, and conducts research in these various areas.
Placebo	Placebo refers to a bogus treatment that has the appearance of being genuine.
Theories	Theories are logically self-consistent models or frameworks describing the behavior of a certain natural or social phenomenon. They are broad explanations and predictions concerning phenomena of interest.
Monoamine theory of depression	The monoamine theory of depression predicts that too much norepinephrine and/or serotonin leads to mania, and too little leads to depression.
Diathesis	A predisposition toward a disease or abnormality is a diathesis.
Adrenal cortex	Adrenal cortex refers to the outer layer of the adrenal glands, which produces hormones that affect salt intake, reactions to stress, and sexual development.
Hormone	A hormone is a chemical messenger from one cell (or group of cells) to another. The best known are those produced by endocrine glands, but they are produced by nearly every organ system. The function of hormones is to serve as a signal to the target cells; the action of the hormone is determined by the pattern of secretion and the signal transduction of the receiving tissue.
Stress hormones	Group of hormones including cortico steroids, that are involved in the body's physiological stress response are referred to as stress hormones.

Anxiety	Anxiety is a complex combination of the feeling of fear, apprehension and worry often accompanied by physical sensations such as palpitations, chest pain and/or shortness of breath.
Anxiety disorder	Anxiety disorder is a blanket term covering several different forms of abnormal anxiety, fear, phobia and nervous condition, that come on suddenly and prevent pursuing normal daily routines.
Hypertension	Hypertension is a medical condition where the blood pressure in the arteries is chronically elevated. Persistent hypertension is one of the risk factors for strokes, heart attacks, heart failure and arterial aneurysm, and is a leading cause of chronic renal failure.
Tachycardia	Tachycardia is an abnormally rapid beating of the heart, defined as a resting heart rate of over 100 beats per minute. Common causes are autonomic nervous system or endocrine system activity, hemodynamic responses, and various forms of cardiac arrhythmia.
Perception	Perception is the process of acquiring, interpreting, selecting, and organizing sensory information.
Amygdala	Located in the brain's medial temporal lobe, the almond-shaped amygdala is believed to play a key role in the emotions. It forms part of the limbic system and is linked to both fear responses and pleasure. Its size is positively correlated with aggressive behavior across species.
Anhedonia	Anhedonia is the inability to experience pleasure from normally pleasurable life events such as eating, exercise, and social/sexual interactions.
Panic attack	An attack of overwhelming anxiety, fear, or terror is called panic attack.
Compulsion	An apparently irresistible urge to repeat an act or engage in ritualistic behavior such as hand washing is referred to as a compulsion.
Obsession	An obsession is a thought or idea that the sufferer cannot stop thinking about. Common examples include fears of acquiring disease, getting hurt, or causing harm to someone. They are typically automatic, frequent, distressing, and difficult to control or put an end to by themselves.
Agoraphobia	An irrational fear of open, crowded places is called agoraphobia. Many people suffering from agoraphobia, however, are not afraid of the open spaces themselves, but of situations often associated with these spaces, such as social gatherings.
Shaping	The concept of reinforcing successive, increasingly accurate approximations to a target behavior is called shaping. The target behavior is broken down into a hierarchy of elemental steps, each step more sophisticated then the last. By successively reinforcing each of the the elemental steps, a form of differential reinforcement, until that step is learned while extinguishing the step below, the target behavior is gradually achieved.
Fraternal twins	Fraternal twins usually occur when two fertilized eggs are implanted in the uterine wall at the same time. The two eggs form two zygotes, and these twins are therefore also known as dizygotic. Dizygotic twins are no more similar genetically than any siblings.
Stimulus	A change in an environmental condition that elicits a response is a stimulus.
Generalized anxiety disorder	Generalized anxiety disorder is an anxiety disorder that is characterized by uncontrollable worry about everyday things. The frequency, intensity, and duration of the worry are disproportionate to the actual source of worry, and such worry often interferes with daily functioning.
Panic disorder	A panic attack is a period of intense fear or discomfort, typically with an abrupt onset and usually lasting no more than thirty minutes. The disorder is strikingly different from other

	types of anxiety, in that panic attacks are very sudden, appear to be unprovoked, and are often disabling. People who have repeated attacks, or feel severe anxiety about having another attack are said to have panic disorder.
Benzodiazepines	The benzodiazepines are a class of drugs with hypnotic, anxiolytic, anticonvulsant, amnestic and muscle relaxant properties. Benzodiazepines are often used for short-term relief of severe, disabling anxiety or insomnia.
Diazepam	Diazepam, brand names: Valium, Seduxen, in Europe Apozepam, Diapam, is a 1,4-benzodiazepine derivative, which possesses anxiolytic, anticonvulsant, sedative and skeletal muscle relaxant properties. Diazepam is used to treat anxiety and tension, and is the most effective benzodiazepine for treating muscle spasms.
Addiction	Addiction is an uncontrollable compulsion to repeat a behavior regardless of its consequences. Many drugs or behaviors can precipitate a pattern of conditions recognized as addiction, which include a craving for more of the drug or behavior, increased physiological tolerance to exposure, and withdrawal symptoms in the absence of the stimulus.
Ataxia	Ataxia is unsteady and clumsy motion of the limbs or trunk due to a failure of the fine coordination of muscle movements.
Tremor	Tremor is the rhythmic, oscillating shaking movement of the whole body or just a certain part of it, caused by problems of the neurons responsible from muscle action.
Insomnia	Insomnia is a sleep disorder characterized by an inability to sleep and/or to remain asleep for a reasonable period during the night.
Animal model	An animal model usually refers to a non-human animal with a disease that is similar to a human condition.
Attention	Attention is the cognitive process of selectively concentrating on one thing while ignoring other things. Psychologists have labeled three types of attention: sustained attention, selective attention, and divided attention.
Syndrome	The term syndrome is the association of several clinically recognizable features, signs, symptoms, phenomena or characteristics which often occur together, so that the presence of one feature indicates the presence of the others.
Tics	Tics are a repeated, impulsive action, almost reflexive in nature, which the person feels powerless to control or avoid.
Personality	Personality refers to the pattern of enduring characteristics that differentiates a person, the patterns of behaviors that make each individual unique.
Coprolalia	Coprolalia is involuntary swearing that is an occasional but rare characteristic of Tourette syndrome patients.
Genitals	Genitals refers to the internal and external reproductive organs.
Epilepsy	Epilepsy is a chronic neurological condition characterized by recurrent unprovoked neural discharges. It is commonly controlled with medication, although surgical methods are used as well.
Basal ganglia	The basal ganglia are a group of nuclei in the brain associated with motor and learning functions.
Hypothesis	A specific statement about behavior or mental processes that is testable through research is a hypothesis.
Basic research	Basic research has as its primary objective the advancement of knowledge and the theoretical understanding of the relations among variables . It is exploratory and often driven by the

	researcher's curiosity, interest or hunch.
Population	Population refers to all members of a well-defined group of organisms, events, or things.
Comparative research	Comparative research is a research methodology that aims to make comparisons across different countries or cultures. A major problem is that the data sets in different countries may not use the same categories, or define categories differently.
Neuroscience	A field that combines the work of psychologists, biologists, biochemists, medical researchers, and others in the study of the structure and function of the nervous system is neuroscience.
Pinel	Pinel is regarded as the father of modern psychiatry. He was a clinician believing that medical truth derived from clinical experience. While at Bicêtre, Pinel did away with bleeding, purging, and blistering in favor a therapy that involved close contact with and careful observation of patients.

Printed in the United Kingdom
by Lightning Source UK Ltd.
123324UK00001B/43/A